Herbert Tichborne

Noqu Talanoa

Stories from the South Seas

Herbert Tichborne

Noqu Talanoa
Stories from the South Seas

ISBN/EAN: 9783337005603

Printed in Europe, USA, Canada, Australia, Japan

Cover: Foto ©Thomas Meinert / pixelio.de

More available books at **www.hansebooks.com**

NOQU TALANOA

STORIES FROM THE SOUTH SEAS

BY

'SUNDOWNER

LONDON

THE EUROPEAN MAIL LIMITED

IMPERIAL BUILDINGS, LUDGATE CIRCUS, E.C.

1896

Price Half-a-Crown

AUTHOR'S PREFACE

MOST of the stories in this volume have already appeared in substance in *The Weekly Telegraph* and *The Colonies and India*, to whose editors I am indebted for the necessary permission to recapitulate the incidents. I dedicate the book with affectionate remembrances to the thousands of coloured friends with whom I had the pleasure of communing during my wanderings among those earthly paradises known vaguely on this side as the South Pacific Islands. I have enjoyed many a breezy talanoa over the yaqona-bowl with those splendid Polynesians, whose genial and kindly natures have always challenged my warmest admiration and gratitude, and I

have published my story—or Noqu Talanoa
—by way of letting the world know what
good souls I think them to be. Forgetting
their sometime waywardness, I shall always
remember their sterling qualities, their
large hearts, their lovable natures, and
their genial humours. My tongue may
cleave to my mouth if ever I cease to sing
the praises of those bright and cheerful
people, whose kindly comradeship, in danger
as in sport, added so much zest and enjoyment to the glorious holiday it was my
privilege to spend among the picturesque
Pacific archipelagos, ' waiting for sundown.'

CONTENTS

VANUA LEVU has its story of Heloise and
Abelard, and a touching story it is in its way.
There is a little mound on a picturesque hillock overlooking the waters of Loa Bay, in
north-eastern Vanua Levu, wherein lie the
bodies of Serua and Maafu, who loved blindly
and were divided in life, and whom death
brought together in a strange and tragic way.
The love-lorn maidens and buoyant youths
in the Buca country make regular pilgrimage
to the classic little mound where the unfortunate lovers rest together after their troubled
lives, and the legend is told by young and
old in the countryside, with that rare elo-
quence and sympathetic pathos which cha-
racterises the Fijians. Serua was the most
beautiful woman ever born to these parts,

B

according to the story. She was the daughter of the Buli of Loa, and was connected with the best families in Buca and Natewa. As she developed into young-womanhood suitors came from far and near, chiefs of high and low degree, Turagas, Bulis, sons of Rokos—and even, it was said, a son of Tui-Cakau had come across the Straits of Somo Somo in one of the royal canoes to pay court to the charming and accomplished daughter of the head of the Loa commune. Serua was high-spirited and particular, it seems, and one and all were refused in turn. At last her fate arrived with the advent of a party of high-toned Tongans, who came to Eastern Fiji on one of their visits to Tui-Cakau's capital at Somo Somo. The waters to the north of Somo Somo Straits, beyond Kioa and along the Buca coast to Koro-I-Vonu and Rambi, are famous for their turtle and shark fishing, and on many occasions the flash young Tongans were brought thither for sport by the young Taviunian chiefs of

Somo Somo. On one of the turtle-hunting trips Maafu happened to visit Loa, where he saw Serua, and the two appear to have fallen in love at first sight, as the saying goes. But Maafu had to go back to Tonga presently with his companions, and he left with the promise that he would return and marry Serua at the next rising of the *balolo*, some six months later. There was no postal or telegraph communication between Fiji and Tonga in those days, so poor Serua spent the interim fretfully enough. Then came the *balolo*, but no sign or word of the young Tongan chief.

Time sped along, and at last came a rumour from Tonga that Maafu had knelt before another goddess, and had abandoned Serua. The young chieftainess took her trouble sadly enough, and it was some time before she could recover anything like her old gaiety. Suitors from all parts of Vanua Levu, Taviuni, Rambi, and even Ovalau still followed the Loa beauty, and at last, in a sort

of despair, Serua consented to marry Ratu
Maiko, a big chief from the Macuata coast.
The marriage meeting was appointed, fatefully
enough, for the next-coming *balolo*, and as the
time approached there was great rejoicing
and extensive preparations, from Na-Gai-Gai
up to Kumbalau, for it was felt that Ratu
Maiko, being a Vanua Levuan and well-
known in the country, would surely be round
from Macuata to claim his bride at the rising
of the big *balolo*. The months passed, and
there came the rising of the *balolo lai-lai*.
All was in readiness for the wedding arrange-
ments on the eve of the big *balolo*, when there
arose a sea-storm such as is only known, as a
rule, in those regions some months after *balolo*
time. As night came on the storm, instead of
abating, grew fiercer, and as Ratu Maiko and
his friends were on the way from the Macuata
coast by way of Udu and Kumbalau Points,
a good deal of excitement arose as to how
the party of voyagers would fare in the sudden stress of weather. The wind rose, as

did the sea, and, as if to add to the general warring of the elements, a fierce thunderstorm struck across Loa Bay. Through the darkness of the night those on the look-out in Loa could see away across the mouth of the bay in the flashes of lightning which burst upon the place at frequent intervals. At last the anxious watchers in one of the flashes sighted a large royal canoe bearing into the bay, and there was general rejoicing, as the craft seemed able to hold her own in the hurricane. As each succeeding flash, however, showed the canoe bearing inwards, the men began to be alarmed at the way in which she was being driven, for her course appeared to be directed towards a nasty piece of coral reef that stretches out towards Kioa from the Diloi side. Everybody wondered, for the reef was well known to Ratu Maiko, as he must have passed the place hundreds of times. But on the canoe sped, and at last, when one of the lightning flashes showed the position of the vessel to the excited people

of Loa, the canoe was smashing to ribbons
on the coral reef, with her sail gone. There
was really nothing to do but await the course
of events, for no canoe could be launched
from Loa in the teeth of the gale then blowing. There was nothing for it but to wait
patiently, 'the men going out and patrolling
the beach with torches, with a view to rescu-
ing any of the canoe party who might succeed
in struggling inshore. After some hours
bodies began to arrive, and one after another
was picked up in the weird gloom of the fag-
end of the awful night. The women-folk
now helped in the search, and naturally
enough Serua joined anxiously in the gruesome quest. At last, while body after body
was being washed up on the beach, a youth
came rushing from a point where he had
found a body, to announce that the chief had
been washed ashore. Serua, mad with
excitement and grief, rushed forward to the
spot, and stooping over the body, pulled the
chief's tangled hair into something like order,

to find, on looking into the dead face, that she had come upon the body of her old flame, Maafu! Serua threw her arms round the body of her lifeless lover, and remained there. When they went to move her later, she too was dead, and instead of a wedding ceremony on the day of the big *balolo* there was a funeral procession to the little hillock outside the town of Loa. Ratu Maiko reached Loa a few days afterwards, having been detained at Udu by the storm ; but whether the ill-fated Maafu had mistaken the year of the *balolo* on which he had made up his mind to marry Serua is not known to the chronicler, and never will be. But it came to be known that he had been steadily true to poor Serua, as she in reality in her heart had been to him. They were divided in life, but were united in death.

LOVE

Love it is, and love alone,
   Makes the world go round and round ;
Love is surely to be known
   Where a woman's to be found.

THUS says the old song-writer, and as women are to be found amongst the fairy islands of the Pacific, so also is love. 'To make love' is a common expression, but we may search over the wide region of books in vain for a prescription for 'making' it. We make it each in our own way, and it comes natural to us. The profession of love in England is one thing, the profession of love amongst the numerous inhabitants of the Pacific archipelagos is another.

They have a custom in one portion of the New Hebrides which is, to say the least of it, unique. In one of the islands there is a large broken gully in the mountains—the Americans call them cañons. At one spot this cañon is about eighty yards across, and on one side, situated near the top of the ridge, there is a large ledge of rock. When a young man has made it right with his inamorata he, on an appointed day, betakes himself to the cañon, in company with large numbers of his friends and friends of his *fiancée*. The girl, being a deeply interested party, acts as a kind of missile-holder to her future lord and master. From the opposite side to the rock-ledge his *tavi*, or task, is to throw a stone on to the ledge. If the stone remain upon the rock the ceremony of marriage is completed. If the stone should roll off, as it very often does, the marriage is deferred for *ten moons*, during which period both candidates for matrimony are debarred from entering upon that holy state. I attended one of those marriages a few years ago. The bridegroom was a smart young fellow, and several remarks were dropped by

the bystanders, to the effect 'that if Nepuka-
taneseri (Nebuchadnezzar) couldn't make a
stone stick on the ledge, nobody could.'
The bride herself complacently smoked my
pipe, without any apparent anxiety, while
preparations were being made for the ceremony. She had evidently the greatest
confidence in her lover's ability to accomplish
the task he had before him. He justified
the confidence by safely lodging the stone
without much effort, and the happy couple
were at once congratulated by their friends
on their union. We adjourned to the village,
and spent the rest of the day round the
kava-bowl, where the general conversation,
naturally enough, turned upon the experiences
of several of those present in their matrimonial efforts. One old fellow, whose hand
had never been blessed with any cunning for
stone-throwing, had made in his time about
a dozen efforts to take unto himself a wife,
but had met with indifferent luck upon each
occasion, and was consequently still a bache-

lor. The life of a bachelor is not, of course, so hard in the New Hebrides as it is in England. The holiday best of a New Hebridean comprises merely a fathom of light cloth thrown round the loins, and called a 'lava-lava.' He is, therefore, never troubled with that universal obstacle to the British bachelor's happiness, the difficulty of getting his buttons sewn on.

In the Fiji Islands the custom obtains of arranging marriages when the parties are in their infancy. Thus, a bright young Fijian lady often becomes engaged when she is two or three years of age.

The Fijian is only happy when a feast is going on. Upon the slightest possible provocation a feast is organised, and so it happens that the betrothal of a young couple is always made the subject of a festival on a large scale. Scores of pigs are slaughtered and deposited in the *lovos*, or ovens, which, half a century ago, were the receptacles of human bodies on similar occasions. Yams are rooted up

by the ton, and the *koro*, or town in which
the feast is held, is kept in a bustle of excitement from sunrise to sunset.

A marriage engagement commenced in
this way, and extending over a period of perhaps twelve or fifteen years, very often comes
to nothing after all.

Sweethearting, or billing and cooing, a-
mongst the Fijians, is a curious feature in
their social customs.   It is decidedly *tabu* to
do any courting within doors.   The gardens
or plantations are the spots held sacred to
Cupid. And the generally approved trysting-
place of lovers is up, high up, amongst the
branches of a bread-fruit tree. Many a score
times have I, walking round a plantation
on a moonlight night, spied couples perched
forty feet from the ground in the bread-
fruit trees, one on each side of the trunk, a
position which comes fairly within the limits
of a Fijian maiden's ideas of modesty. The
custom is held to have many advantages by
those who indulge in it. Foremost and most

important of these is that you can 'see the old man coming' a good way off. I have never heard, however, any calculation made of the chances one would have if the 'old man' proved to be a 'sticker,' and took up his station at the foot of the tree before one could get down. There is one thing—a man 'up a tree' in Fiji, especially a bread-fruit tree, could stand a long siege without starving.

I have never seen, during years of travel in many countries, a race of people of higher moral instincts than the Fijians. A scandal is of rare occurrence. But the Fijian mother is a born matchmaker, and the Fijian maiden is herself a keen prospector after any good thing in the shape of a matrimonial alliance. While I was trading amongst them, and spending money freely with them, I was—so I afterwards learned—notwithstanding an uncomely personal appearance, generally looked upon as a 'good catch.' It may be necessary to mention here that very many

.of the white residents of Fiji are married to native wives. The ladies in most cases, of course, are daughters of high chiefs, and have been liberally educated. I was one day entertaining a number of young ladies from the house of a neighbouring chief, who was a native magistrate, and with whom I stood upon close official and intimate terms. One of the girls—a tidy soul—was constantly brushing down the table or sweeping the floor. Some of the others twitted her about it. I broke in with a little banter. 'Wait till Lavinia and I are married,' I said, 'and we shall have a servant to keep the house tidy.' My horror may be imagined when, a few days later, the girl, in company with her mother, landed at my door with her baggage ! She had taken me at my word, and I had some heavy work before me to clear the matter up satisfactorily.

The apathy which is engendered by these long marriage engagements among the Fijians is sometimes followed with amusing results.

A young fellow living in my neighbourhood
had been engaged to a girl for about fourteen
years. As neither party had been attracted
by any more fascinating third person, the
long engagement was about to end in a
matrimonial alliance. Accordingly a day was
fixed for the celebration, -and preparations
made for the usual festivities. The appointed
day came round in due course, and the pig
tribe suffered in the usual alarming degree.
The bride and her friends were on hand,
but the bridegroom was *non est.* The day
passed—the festival was partaken of, notwithstanding the non-performance of the
ceremony which occasioned it ; but still 'he
came not.' Next day, however, he appeared,
and was considerably surprised to hear of the
trouble he had occasioned. He had forgotten
all about the wedding business, and had
merely gone for a day's fishing! But he
received such a lesson from his mother-in-
law that was to be, in good round Fijian
(and a fine language it is to abuse a person

with), that he is likely to be more punctual in attending to business connected with her family for the future.

The national beverage in Fiji is the *yaqona*, or *kava*. This is a small tree (*Macropiper methysticum*), the root of which is chewed, and then dissolved in water. After a little straining, to remove the root-dregs, the mixture is fit for drinking. It is an intoxicant, and if the root happens to be old it has a powerful effect. The effect of a yaqona 'drunk' is most peculiar. While the head of the subject remains clear enough to discuss the toughest political question, the legs totally refuse to do their accustomed work. A drunken man is often compelled to hold on to the grass for support. The young girls are invariably employed in the work of grog-chewing when a company sits down to drink. But when you see a young woman chewing grog single-handed for a solitary young man, you know that that couple are engaged to be married. It is one of the best signs that a young woman will make a suitable wife for a youth when she can chew his grog to the proper strength. There are, of course, many differences of taste—some like it 'over proof,' and others prefer it 'under.'

Like the men, the Fijian women comb their hair straight upwards. It stands up stiff like the top of a well-trimmed hedge, and when flowers are to hand, they are profusely planted on top, making the woman to appear as if she carried a miniature flower-garden on the top of her head. A lock of hair on the right temple is preserved, however, for a downward course, and this is carefully plaited and allowed to hang down the side of the cheek. When the girl is married this lock is shorn and never allowed to appear again. Hence the experienced eye can quickly discern the married from the single when a village is entered.

In Samoa when a woman is married several tattoo marks are inflicted upon her. And,

c

both in Fiji and Samoa, the birth of each
child is registered by a tattoo mark on the
mother's hand.   When you see a woman
with her hand covered with these marks you
may be sure she has contributed largely to
the population of her country.   It would have
warmed the heart of Bonaparte to see a
venerable old lady who lives on Vanua Levu.
Her hand is as 'black as sin.'   I was bidding
her 'Good-bye' one day.   '*I veca?*' I asked
as I held her hand.   '*Rua-saga-vulu ka lima*'
(twenty-five), she answered proudly.

In the Society Islands (Tahiti) tattooing
is carried on to an amazing extent.   Serious
crimes are punished by the infliction of a
mark upon the forehead, which, of course, it
is impossible to conceal or efface.   No felon's
mark was ever so terrible in its punishing
effects as this.   The bearer of it is shunned
by everyone, the 'brand of Cain' is literally
upon his brow, and the only peaceful retreat
left to him is the grave.

A CANNIBAL KING, CAKO-BAU, HIGH LORD OF FIJI

EPENESERI, or Ebenezer, Cako-Bau, King of Fiji, Controller of the Sharks, and ' Boss of all the Islands in the World,' was born about a hundred years ago. The exact date is not known, but the traditions are unanimous on the point that the heavens and earth were seriously disturbed and convulsed at the birth of the future prodigy. Gales blew and storms raged. Probably the people had enough to do to look after their houses and canoes, without going to the trouble of fixing a date for the birth of their new Prince.

Tanoa, the father of Cako-Bau, was rather a good King in his way. He was an active man, fond of the chase, of war, and such like manly occupations, while he was, at the same

time, little given to gourmandising. Hence
we find that Tanoa only ordered a man to
be killed and cooked when he wanted a feed ;
he didn't have beef lying about all over the
place, going to waste, as did his predecessors
and the son who succeeded him.

Tanoa is the name given to the large
wooden bowl in which the yaqona, or native
grog, is prepared. The old King had such
a happy way of absorbing yaqona that he
was facetiously called a Tanoa. The name
stuck to him, and he eventually ruled under
it, and handed it down to posterity as the
name of a king who was distinguished from
the rest of his dynasty by the mercifulness of
his character and the wisdom of his reign.
His mercy and wisdom of course grew out
of his economical habits, in that he never
killed more men than he could use.

When Cako-Bau (evil to Bau) was five
years of age he clubbed his first man ! The
victim was tied up in the usual way, a club
given to the boy, who beat the poor

wretch to death, taking, however, about two hours to complete the task. It will be allowed that this was an early age at which to receive his baptism of massacre.

They had a rule or custom in Fiji that when a king or chief died, his wives (and sometimes he had many) were put to death and buried along with him. When Tanoa died he left five widows, Cako-Bau's mother being amongst them. The young King assumed the reins of power immediately upon the death of his father, and his first act was to carry out the usual festivities in connection with the funeral, and the massacre of the widows. Two white missionaries, with their wives and families, lived on Bau at this time, and they made every effort to induce Cako-Bau to spare the women's lives. They annoyed him very much over the matter. 'Why,' he said, 'if I were to omit the observance of such an important custom the people would be justified in telling me that I was unfit to rule over them.'

The ceremony was carried out accordingly, Cako-Bau leading off the massacre by strangling his own mother.

For many years after his accession to the throne of Bau the career of King Cako-Bau was one long array of cowardly massacre and unjust wars. The whole of the Fijian Archipelago, which consists of about two hundred islands, became subject to him, and he ruled them with a hand of iron. But white people began to gather round him, and the King at last commenced to find that it was necessary for him to exercise more care in the discharge of his royal functions. Many of the leading nations had consuls at Levuka. The American Consul always had the ' stars and stripes ' flying over his official residence. A Fijian from the Livoni Valley was in the Levuka one night, and an idea occurred to him that the Yankee colours would make a picturesque and comfortable sulu (a waist-cloth—the one article of a Fijian's wearing apparel). Accordingly, in the morning the

Consul was surprised to find the old flag gone. He went down to Cako-Bau and lodged a formal complaint. The King only laughed at him. The Consul used considerable language of a parliamentary character, and let the matter lie over for a while. Some time afterwards, an American man-of-war entered the port. The Consul made a due representation of matters, with the result that Cako-Bau was carried aboard, and informed that he would not be allowed to return to shore till the flag stealer was produced. Of course the King immediately sent emissaries into the Livoni, and they returned in a few days with the culprit. He was flogged, and he and Cako-Bau were then allowed to depart. The Americans were satisfied, but the King had a bone to pick with the man whose offence had caused His Majesty to be subjected to indignity. The man was slowly tortured to death in the public square at Totoga in Levuka. His arm was first cut off at the elbow, and thrown into the oven; in fact, he was dismembered by slow degrees, and the King feasted upon him.

The first thing which began to show some likelihood of interfering seriously with the rule of Cako-Bau in Fiji was the rising power of Maafu, in the Lau, or eastern group. Maafu has been called the 'Lord Byron of Tonga,' which country he had been compelled to leave some years before. He was one of the cleverest native chiefs who ever came to the surface in the Pacific, and his untimely death at Lakeba a few years ago was universally deplored. Maafu was an extensive trader, had amassed a large sum of money, and possessed many ships. Finding from the disturbed state of the country that it was necessary for the proper protection of his business and his property that he should keep a small army, he equipped one, which grew in time to formidable dimensions.

Cako-Bau quarrelled with Maafu at last, and the latter would probably have smashed the Bau ruler were it not for British intervention and the subsequent annexation of Fiji to this country.

If Maafu had lived, he would have succeeded, upon the death of his uncle, the late King George of Tonga, to the throne of that country.

During the latter portion of Cako-Bau's reign he had the assistance of a white Ministry in his councils. Like administrations in England, the King's Ministers went in and out, but their removal from office was generally the effect of a cause different to that which removes an English Government. One Ministry, I remember, in which a friend of mine held the portfolio of Chancellor of the Exchequer, lost office through having purchased ten cases of gin of inferior quality for His Majesty's use. The old man was not to be humbugged with cheap gin, so he sent for the Leader of the Opposition and charged him with the commission of forming a new Government.

The Administration resolved upon a
great coronation ceremony. All the leading
chiefs of the group were called together at
Levuka to witness the ceremony. A daïs
was erected, and the crown manufactured.
The man who made the crown still lives in
Fiji, and he always complains that he was
never paid the half-sovereign which he was
promised for making the article. On the
other hand, it appears that Cako-Bau was
not satisfied with the workmanship. The
coronation ceremony took place, and late in
the day Cako-Bau stuck his penknife into
the velvet covering by which the hard
material of the crown was concealed. This
material he found to consist of part of a
kerosene tin, and his disgust was great.
The old man flung the crown from him with
some very strong and unregal expressions
indeed. The Administration which con-
ceived the coronation idea was ignominiously dismissed from office.

When I remember that popular term in

use amongst us, *De mortuis nil nisi bonum*, I begin to fear that, in speaking roughly of Cako-Bau, I may be making a breach in what has come to be a generally recognised law. But there is some excuse for me in the recollection that the old King himself spoke at times very depreciatingly of the dead. We learn that he constantly interrupted the decorum of a banquet by flinging a piece of bokola (dead man) from him, with an oath about the ' toughness ' or the ' saltiness ' of the deceased.

What a victory the good Christian missionaries scored when they succeeded in changing this human fiend into the fine character which he exhibited during the latter portion of his life !

Cako-Bau resisted Christianity for many years. He, however, was good enough to allow the missionaries a footing in the country, but no particular respect was paid to them. On Bau, the Fijian capital, white missionaries had been allowed a residence from the time of Tanoa, the predecessor of Cako-Bau. But the only spot upon which they were allowed to erect a residence was upon the rubbish heap in the centre of the town. Here two of them lived for many years, with their wives and families, witnesses very often of the cannibal feasts for which Bau was notorious.

The good King George of Tonga was the man who eventually succeeded in prevailing upon Cako-Bau to embrace Christianity

The old man certainly could never be blamed for doing things by halves. From a cut-throat and cannibal of advanced ideas, he turned right round to a God-fearing, humane Christian. He abandoned polygamy, as well as the 'bokola' trade, and put forth his influence amongst the different tribes in the group in the assistance of the missionaries.

Towards his latter days he also adopted the more civilised custom of wearing shirts

and trousers regularly, although they
'scratched' him a good deal at first. When
the King visited Sydney, in 1874, he was
the guest of Sir Hercules Robinson, the then
Governor of New South Wales. His
Majesty interviewed a George Street tailor,
who promptly turned him out in a neat-fitting
dress suit. Immediately after his first dinner
at Government House the old man retired,
and was not seen again for some hours. He
was subsequently unearthed in the kitchen.
The dress suit had been abandoned, and the
conventional Fijian sulu substituted for it.
The potentate had extemporised the sulu
from a table-cloth, and had comfortably set
himself out for a smoke in the kitchen. He
wore that damask sulu for a long time after,
its great advantage over the dress suit being
that it 'didn't scratch!'

CANNIBALISM

LANDING once upon the coast of Malayta, one of the Solomon Islands, the first sight which riveted my attention was the body of a little girl lying under a cocoa-nut tree, with a spear stuck partly through its head. A crowd of natives stood near, engaged apparently in some festal business, but nobody appeared to heed the child. It was yet alive, and its cries for 'mother' and for a 'drink of water' made an impression upon me which is with me yet. I instinctively drew my revolver. A man is sometimes prompted to attempt foolish things in emergencies of such a nature as this.

I happened to be known to some of the people present. A young Christoval chief approached me and told me in a friendly way

to put the ' shooter ' away. I managed afterwards, however, with his assistance, to save
the poor child from the oven, for a time, at
least.

Any inclination I had for saving victims
was useless in the next case which came before me, further up the village. The candidate for *pièce de résistance* honours here
was a full-grown warrior, who had, I learnt
upon inquiry, been trying the 'John Hamp-
den' business, and had encountered some
bad luck in the venture. He was as dead as
the proverbial door nail, and was tied up and
properly hamstrung, awaiting the preparation
of the *lovo*, or oven, which was to receive
him. I hope the English reader will not be
too much horrified when I mention that I was
subsequently invited to partake of the re-
freshments at the banquet which followed.
I hope it will also be needless to mention
that the offer was refused. But for the
offence of saying these horrible things, I may
be allowed to congratulate English people

upon the fact that such scenes may now be reckoned amongst the things that were, and to go a little further in stating the universally acknowledged fact that the English people are solely responsible for their discontinuance.

It is but a few years, comparatively speaking, since the English missionary hoisted his glorious flag in the Pacific, but to say that the traveller to the Islands to-day is astonished when he views and realises the work which has been accomplished, is not saying enough—he is amazed. The American Consul at Levuka, a few years ago (he has since been compelled to make way for the *protégé* of a friend of President Cleveland's) had a curious relic in his office with which to edify his visitors. This consisted of the fork of a vesi tree, in which were embedded about a hundred shin-bones, arm-bones, jaw-bones, and other fragments of the human frame. The tree from which the fork had been taken stood underneath a rock-ledge or precipice in the Livoni Mountains, on top of which was situated a favourite feasting ground. These bones were merely a few of those which had been thrown over from time to time, and had happened to catch in the fork of the tree. I remember saying to the Consul once : ' There must have been a considerable pile of bones around the foot of the tree where this came from ?' 'Aye,' said the Consul, 'you kin bet there just was—*con*-siderable !'

The Maoris of New Zealand were at one time cannibals of no mean order. The hot springs and lakes in different parts of the North Island were, from an early date, much valued by the Maoris for their curative pro-perties. They were the subject of many a dispute and many a war between the different tribes. On the conclusion of a battle in the neighbourhood of one of these boiling springs the prisoners of war were thrown by the victors into the natural boiling cauldrons, and subsequently eaten. A rule existed amongst

some of the tribes which allowed every
warrior to use his own victims himself.   His
wife and children, even his mother-in-law,
were not allowed to partake of the repast.

There is one chief of the Arawa tribe—
the Arawas dwelt in the Hot Lake district,
the scene of the recent volcanic disturbances
—who is mentioned a good deal in Maori
history.   Space will not allow me to give his
name.   But the meaning of one of his titles
was—' Eater of his own relations!'   He
appears to have been a kind of Home Ruler,
and made a considerable mark in the history
of his time.   In curious contrast to this chief,
however, was a warrior of the same tribe, a
contemporary of his, who, though a valiant
fighter and a slayer of many scores of people,
possessed a strange disinclination for
' tangata,' or man, when dished up.   This
eccentricity on his part lost him prestige, and
he failed to advance himself much politically ;
the only circumstance which warrants the
retention of his name in history being his

unaccountable aversion to the favourite
national meat of his country.

'Tangata' is the Maori pronunciation of
the Fijian word 'tamata,' which is the synonym for our word 'man.' A dead man, however, is called by the Fijians a 'bokola,' but
this did not prevent a wag in Suva from
passing the remark once that the Fijians
were very fond of *tamatas*. Through the
prevalence of cannibalism in New Zealand in
the old days, and the custom of preserving
the heads of the victims, a great trade in
skulls arose with the advent of the first white
settlers. The trade remained brisk for some
years, but the custom of cannibalising died
out, and heads eventually became scarce.
We learn in one of the published histories of
New Zealand of a trader who had been applied
to for some skulls replying, ''Eds is 'eds
now, sir; 'eds is wery scarce, sir, I can assure
you.'

The decadence of the custom did not,

however, prevent the Australian colonies from being inundated with Maori skulls. When I was a young fellow I remember taking part in an amateur representation of Hamlet. We purchased a Maori skull from an old store-keeper in the town for a shilling to represent poor Yorick's. It tickled us a good deal at the time to see the skull of a wild Maori doing duty for the jester's, but we have lived and learned since. Not so very long ago I saw the head of a notorious murdering bush-ranger apostrophised by the Prince of Denmark, ' Alas, poor Yorick ! I knew him once.' One of the most notorious cases of the consumption of a white man by cannibals was that of the Rev. Mr. Baker, a missionary in Fiji. Mr. Baker performed some noble pioneering work in that country, and in 1868 he started upon an expedition, in company with some native Christians, into the mountains of Viti Levu. Taking a kind of passport from the ruling chief in the Rewa River district, Mr. Baker travelled a considerable distance up the Rewa, and struck into the Namosi Valley. He entered a village at last, outside the borders of the Christian district at the time. He was, with his companions, most hospitably entertained by the villagers during the night, and on the following morning he took his departure, little dreaming of any treachery. As a matter of fact, however, the chief, who had arranged for his protection along the road, had turned traitor, and sent word along after him to the Namosi people not to let him proceed. They construed the message into a mandate for the 'removal' of the missionary in the orthodox way, with the club.

Mr. Baker and his people were proceeding along a track or 'wakolo,' accompanied by some of the villagers, one of whom walked immediately in front of him. This man suddenly stepped aside from the path, allowing Baker to pass him. As the missionary passed the native struck him on the head with his club, and that part of the ceremony was concluded. Another ceremony followed, when the body was cooked and eaten.

Many of the people who had a hand in this affair are alive yet, and, of course, well known. They invariably, however, deny having partaken of the ' bokola-na-papalagi.' On the top waters of the Rewa I once encountered an old scoundrel who took a leading part in the affair. I was in the company of a gentleman who has lived for many years in the group, and who has had a large experience amongst the natives. We questioned the old fellow about his connection with Baker's affair. He denied any complicity in it. Later on, over a tanoa of yaqona, my friend said to him, ' I have heard that the *bokola ko Misi Peka* (Mr. Baker's body) was very salt to the taste ; not like a *bokola na Vaka Viti* (Fijian body) ? ' ' Don't you believe it,' said the old man unguardedly ; ' there wasn't a bit of difference.'

Did the reader ever hear the story of ' Cook's club ' ? A visitor once went to Bar-

num's celebrated show in New York. He
was looking about a good deal, evidently in
search of some relic. An attendant asked
him at last if there was anything which he
was anxious to find. Yes, there was, he
said. He wanted to gaze upon the club that
killed Captain Cook! The attendant had
never heard of it himself, but he sought the
'boss,' the great showman himself, and mentioned the matter to him. Barnum also,
strangely enough, had never heard of it, but
he was not going to allow anyone to leave
Barnum's show without being able to see any
relic that could be mentioned. A club was
taken privily from a case, and a ticket,
'Cook's club,' hastily pasted upon it. The
visitor was then invited to come and see it.
'Ah,' he said, when he looked upon it, 'I
thought you would be sure to have it here.
I have been in all the other small shows in
town, and they have got it, so I sorter
reckoned that Barnum's would not be without it.'

It is necessary to have heard about Cook's club to understand the phenomenal relic which is popularly treasured in Fiji. ' Baker's fork ' they call it. This is the fork with which the body of poor Mr. Baker was eaten. I have myself seen about two hundred and fifty, and of course there are many hundreds which I have not seen. Everybody has it. The traveller to Fiji is invariably sold the real ' Baker's fork.' I bought one myself once for half a dollar, but the burst of laughter which greeted me when I produced it at my hotel in Levuka made me ponder, and I was glad soon to abandon the treasure. I had, however, a consoling friend in the hotel-keeper, who observed that it ' was two bob clean throw'd away ! '

TALANOA NA YAQONA.[1]

THERE is one thing which forcibly strikes the traveller among the different peoples who inhabit the earth, and that is the undeniable propensity of the human race generally for indulgence in some kind of intoxicating liquor. The national beverage in this part of the world appears to be beer, or ' Ye fine olde nutt browne ale,' whilst the Continental peoples have of late years to a great extent dropped the ' bier' for the less harmful *vino* of Southern Europe. In different parts of Asia *arak* and *samshu* hold first place in the hearts of the drinking people ; whilst in Africa many decoctions from the popular

[1] The freest English synonym for *talanoa* is *a tale* ; *yaqona* is Fijian for *grog*. ' Talanoa na yaqona ' is the title given to the much-honoured custom of indulging in a conversation round the grog-bowl.

coco-nut and from mealie grain are used for 'stealing away the brains' of the people.

In the South Sea Islands the most generally approved drink is the yaqona, or kava. In some groups, however, the *Macropiper methysticum*, or yaqona root, is not indigenous, and a toddy is made from the coco-nut. This toddy, or tekereri, as it is called by the Line islanders—the people who enjoy a monopoly of its use—is much used by European residents in the Islands, who call it South Sea champagne. The method of procuring it from the coco-nut tree is simple. The native climbs a tree upon which the young nuts are beginning to make their appearance. The nuts are scraped off, and the young branch which held them is 'docked' with a knife and inserted in a bottle. The bottle is tied on and left to hang. In about twelve hours it is full of the future tekereri, when it is removed and another put in its place. The toddy is then allowed to stand for another twelve hours or so, by which time it is fermented, and is fit for use. When allowed to stand for two or three days tekereri is a violent intoxicant, but when taken in the ordinary way, about twelve hours after abstraction from the tree, its exhilarating qualities are about on a par with ordinary Australian or European wine.

The Line islander, of whom there are a large number on the plantations in Fiji, is a firm believer in his tekereri. Every man on a plantation has to be allowed his own tree. The unrestricted use of the toddy very often, of course, leads to serious trouble, as these people are naturally very ferocious in their habits. Many horrible murders which have occurred in Fiji during late years are directly attributable to the tekereri sprees.

The drink for the gods, however, in the Pacific Islands, is yaqona. What the good Rhine wine is to the German baron, so is the flowing bowl of yaqona to the South Sea chief. The effect of a few bowls of yaqona is very soothing. It produces a feeling

somewhat akin to that pictured by the
Arizona cow-boy who was once treated to a
blow-out of Mononghela whisky. 'Arter the
vi-ands wur got through,' he said, 'the liquors
wur brought in. An' wot liquors they wuz,
too! They warn't none o' thet kind ez
made yer feel like hittin' yer mother, an'
flyin' round an' smashin' things ginirally;
they wuz just thet kind as made yer feel like
histin' up yer glars sorter genteel-like, an'
sayin', "Joe, ole pard, I'm lookin' at yer."'

I shall never forget that feeling of happy
contentment which pervades the senses when
we have thrown ourselves upon the mats
round the *tanoa*, or grog-bowl, after partaking
of the solid portion of a chief's hospitality.

The matter of form command of a chief
is invariably given out after dinner, when all
hands are expected to come round the tanoa
and join in the talanoa na yaqona. The con-
versational powers of the average Fijian are
of no mean order. And what is generally
said of the Maori may often with equal truth

be said of the Fijian—he is a born orator.
The reader can imagine the keenness of the
interest felt by the average new chum as he
listens to the graphic description of a can-
nibalistic orgie, in which, perchance, the
narrator has taken a leading and important
part.   When I was on Vanua Levu I was
one evening the guest of old Tui Kama
(King Kama), the ruler of the Buca district.
The Tui was telling us of a war in which he
had taken part in Buca some years previously.
' Those ovens near my door were full of men
for several days,' said the old chief, 'and that
grey-headed old fellow over there '—pointing
to a benevolent-looking individual who was
just in the act of drinking a bowl of yaqona
—' that old fellow partook of portions of nine
different men during the solevu (feast) which
followed the war.'   The old fellow alluded to
hastily stopped in the middle of his drink (it
may be mentioned that in a general way the
Fijian only stops between the start and finish
of a bowl of grog when he is interrupted by

an earthquake) to correct his chief. ' Segai,' he said, ' Koi au sa mamau *tinie-ka-dua* na bokola.' (' Nay, I ate of *eleven* bodies on that occasion !') The Tui promptly apologised. There is a good deal of the courtier about a Fijian chieftain.

In Fiji the yaqona is prepared by the chewing process. Some white people, however, who are unable to use the chewed article, have it grated, but the devotee will as soon drink water as the grated grog. Grating does not bring the flavour or the essence out properly. But the white drinking population of Fiji were much troubled recently by some inquiries made by Sir William Mac-Gregor, when he was Chief Medical Officer of the group, into the grog-chewing business. The doctor took three ounces of the ordinary yaqona root. This was given to a young woman, who chewed it in the usual way. After the chewing process was completed the result was weighed. The three ounces had developed into eight—a palpable gain of five ounces. The question of the composition of this surplus five ounces of 'grog' was invariably allowed to stand over till next sitting.

A Fijian is properly equipped for the road when he has a few leaves of tobacco stuck behind his ear—as a store clerk carries his pen—and a root of grog in his hand. If he meets an acquaintance, or a stranger for that matter, a leaf of the fragrant weed is exchanged, and an adjournment made for liquid refreshment. He will scarcely ever, or, in fact, never, meet a countryman who is not prepared to join him in a drink.

On Savage Island, where the root is not found, but where the rites of hospitality are as highly respected as they are in the Western Archipelagos, the man who is desirous of 'standing treat' invites his friend to join him in a pig. A pig, or *vuaka* as he is called in the South Seas—evidently the native rendition of the word *porker*—requires to be an old pig if two ordinary natives can't finish him. Hence a Savage Islander is often heard to say, in refusing a proffered drink, or rather pig, ' You must really excuse me this time, for I have already had about seven vuakas this morning, and begin to feel full up.'

There is a wide difference between going on a spree on pig and indulging heavily in yaqona. There is one point of affinity, how-ever—the over-indulgence in either luxury is productive of a certain amount of discomfort. If you have ever seen an injudicious and misguided young puppy dog who has just emerged from an encounter with a well-filled dish of milk, the remembrance of it will assist you in framing a mental picture of a Savage Islander who has just arrived home drunk!

A drunken man is often said ' to have the devil in him.' If the devils or evil spirits had not been driven from the swine in years gone by, I wonder how many devils the satiated Savage Islander would have in him!

Talking of Savage Island reminds me for a moment of a visit I paid to it some years since. The jolly old skipper in whose company I was brought a case of gin ashore to treat the King. The liquor was consumed by an early hour in the evening ; and, the old King having retired, we accepted an offer from one of his numerous young-blood relations to have a cruise round the town. My friend the skipper, being an ordinary kind of seafaring man, was unlike most of the skippers we read about in books, and had partaken freely of the gin while it lasted. In true sailor fashion he succeeded in getting both of us into trouble. We were detained ashore all night on parole. The following morning a sort of judicial inquiry was solemnly held into our conduct. The King himself tried the cause, dressed in a volunteer's pants with red stripes down the sides, a dress coat with one of the tails torn off, and a tall white hat. Shoes and shirt were alike wanting. His Majesty, after long consideration, decided to inflict a fine upon the captain. We asked how much ? This delayed the proceedings

E

for a considerable time longer. At last a young fellow—an ovisa, or officer—approached and asked the captain to produce all the money he had upon him. This was done, with the result that $18 were placed on the table. I was then invited to do likewise. I produced my bank—$43. The two lots were carefully put together, counted, and recounted, and the King informed of the total amount, when he gravely settled the proceedings by recording a fine of $61 against the captain. Need I say that the fine was paid? The captain, however, displayed wonderful alacrity in devising what he exultantly termed a method of revenge. We had a busy day on board our schooner, opening cases of gin, removing capsules from the bottles, and watering the otherwise pure liquid. In the experience of the previous evening the King had developed an extraordinary taste for yaqona-na-papalagi (white man's grog); his craving for it had to be satisfied, and hang the expense. Our experience of the morning

suggested the necessity of a sudden and sub-
stantial rise in the price of our liquor (we
were traders then). To make a long story
short, we soon had our dollars back again,
as trade was brisk for the next few days.

I am afraid we were very wicked. But
our evil doings had a good effect on the mind
of the King. A trader who subsequently
visited the island got into a trouble somewhat
similar to ours. He was dragged to the
tribunal of justice, but the fine registered
against him was two cases of gin. That was
a less roundabout plan of the King's for
attaining a certain result.

THE 'GODS' IN FIJI

HAs there ever been a people who have been without a god ? There is a want—a craving—in the human breast generally for the protection and comfort of something beyond the stars. It has often occurred to me that the fear of death may account in a great measure for this human phenomenon. Where Christianity has not reached people you will invariably find a god of some sort to whom they look. They have some imposing gods in Africa and Asia. The followers of Mahomet, of Brahmin, of Confucius are legion. They have big gods in these parts, but not many of them.

In the South Seas, however, the gods are generally of a much smaller order and much less influential. It has a sadly depreciating

influence on the god business when the
Pacific believer can see, almost any day he
likes, a British heathen enter a 'relic' shop
in Sydney or Melbourne and purchase a
South Sea Island god, right out, for a few
shillings.

The god is very often made of wood, and
in islands where hard wood is scarce they do
not devote much wood to his manufacture.
In some parts of the Solomons he is cut out
to very small lengths indeed, and in many
cases the workmanship is of a poor order. I
gave a hard-up Solomon Islander half a dollar
once for a god who had done considerable
service in his time. He had given the people
rain when they wanted it, and had been very
obliging in many respects. They had on
some occasions asked him to do tough jobs,
which he failed to carry out, but this was
generally attributed to the wicked character
of the persons who had preferred the pray-
erful requests. Accordingly he had main-
tained his popularity for a considerable time,

and in fact would have been ruling yet were it not for the advent of Christianity. The missionaries settled him, and after the lapse of time he fell into my hands. He is very ugly, and I may say candidly that I have no faith in him as a god. The man who manufactured him in the Solomons died, so I heard upon inquiry, a natural death. If I had been a god, with the powers that he had, the man who made me should have died a most sudden and awful death. But he would be of little use in England, seeing that he was more in the line of a 'rain god' than anything else. The kind of god I should like to bring to England would be an anti-rain god. If he were *sound* what a business we could do!

In Fiji I encountered a strong illustration of the powerful effect of cradle teaching upon the mind. We remember what our mothers have taught us.

The tribes of the district in which I lived at the time had a god who lived underground.

He was a tremendous size, and everything around him was proportionately big. His day was about 500 years long, and the night a similar length. For the past two or three hundred years he had been in bed, having his ordinary night's rest. He was a good god, of course, who went to bed at sunset, and didn't go fooling round taverns for 250 years or so, spending the best part of his night drinking yaqona and discussing local politics. He did very little for his people, as far as they could remember ; but then, how can you expect a god to attend to business when he is in bed? I know I should be sorry to wake him to listen to my prayers.

He has been very restless of late years, turning about a good deal in bed. Every one of these turns produces a shock of earthquake upon the top. I have had the honour of being disturbed and alarmed by two of these turns. Many of the old people, of course, believe in this god still. They hope he won't get up early in the morning, for when he stands up Fiji is likely to go up too. He is not going to allow Fiji to be overrun with white people, and a Christian god rammed down the throats of his people when he can prevent it by bursting up the whole concern. Did not a Maori god of Tongariro go along the underground track a few years ago and blow the pink and white terraces of Roto-mahana all to smash, because the conduct of his people in holding communion with the white man had seriously annoyed him ? But to revert for a moment to the influence of cradle teaching. I had an old Fijian in my employ once who had been *lotu*, or Christian, for many years. The missionaries had converted him from a worshipper of the underground god into a zealous worshipping Christian. He took very ill, and he was about to die. I spoke to him one evening about his prospects, and suggested that I would send over for the missionary for him on the following morning. He declined the

offer in the most emphatic way. He had
been thinking the matter over, he said, since
he had been taken ill, and had come to the
conclusion that the white man's God was
only humbug after all. White men had only
gone to Fiji to make money—not to save the
souls of the heathen. And, besides, he had
never seen or heard anything of the Christian
God. But his old god, about whom his
mother had told him often, testified to his
presence by these shocks of earthquake. ' He
doesn't do much for us,' the old man continued,
' but he lets us know he's about.' I tried
in vain to make him receive the missionary,
but he was obdurate, and died without him.
And before he died he called his people
about him, and troubled them a good deal
with warnings to abandon the Christian God.
The missionary had some work for a while
after repairing the damage.

In the Straits of Somo Somo, between
Vanua Levu and Taviuni, dwells the great
water god of northern Fiji, *Daka-waqa* (keel

of a canoe). Daka-waqa is a shark of
tremendous size, who is thus called because
when seen in the water his appearance
resembled that of an overturned canoe. He
has one residence underneath the island of
Benau, opposite Vuna Point, and another in
a cave up the Buca River, about twenty
miles further up the coast of Vanua Levu, a
sort of Windsor and Balmoral, as it were.
There is a large native graveyard on Benau,
where many thousands of people have been
buried at different times. The old custom
was to drive a great stake into the grave
a few days after a burial. This gave the
devil a chance to depart from the body, and
so leave it clear and in a fit state to be
adopted by Daka-waqa. Sometimes an old
sinner died, and it was a difficult task for
the medicine man to get the devil out of him.
In a tough case of this kind, when the devil
happened to prove obdurate, the matter was
generally referred to Daka-waqa himself, who,
upon the receipt of a small fee, in the shape

of a baby, thrown into the sea where he could get it, promptly settled the business by driving that particular devil away to the farthest ends of the earth. Benau was *tabu* against him for ever. His body-snatching games in that district were at an end. I once had a long talk with an old believer in Daka-waqa. The god's superiority to the Christian God commended itself to the old man from the circumstance that he did not allow any devil to get the better of him. The Christian God was altogether too mild a character. The old fellow couldn't realise how a God of His reputed power could allow a devil to set up a business in opposition to Him, and do more work in one year in the collection of souls than God Himself appeared to do in a thousand! Some years ago, when I lived in the Straits of Somo Somo, the appearance of Daka-waqa in the Buca River one day caused great consternation amongst the people. I, in my ordinary heathenish way, determined to force an interview with

him if possible. I had some Solomon
Islanders with me who were as much
heathen as myself as far as Daka-waqa was
concerned. We blocked the bar on the
mouth of the river with bamboos, and gave
chase up the river in a *takia*, or small canoe.
We were not long in finding him, but the
Solomons were afraid to take to the water
after him. He was far and away the biggest
gio (shark) they had ever encountered.
Accordingly I had to satisfy myself with
sending an occasional bullet after him when
we managed to cross him. I must have hit
him hard at last, for he made down stream
at a terrific rate, and managed to break away
through our bamboo fence before we could
reach him. That was the last occasion in
recent years in which the Daka-waqa has
been seen. After my sacrilegious treatment
of him he will probably be as anxious to rid
the country of white men as his godly brother
the underground divinity. The god of the
leeward coast of Viti Levu (Big Fiji) is called

Na Droga (the Growler). He only came amongst the people upon one occasion, many years ago. He was in appearance like an ordinary white man, and he spoke in a language somewhat similar to that most in use amongst rough English sailor men. When a sailor is annoyed and commences to use some of those popular seafaring phrases which generally come under the heading of 'stormy language,' the natives say that he is talking like Na Droga. The missionaries have done the cause of Na Droga considerable harm by suggesting that he was no god at all, but more probably a shipwrecked sailor !

Dengei, the great serpent god, had his location in the neighbourhood of the Tai-Levu and Bau coasts. He was a sea-god, but he occasionally condescended to come ashore for a short spell, generally to have a 'yaqona drink' with the medicine man, and to express his admiration of the doctor's house and its furniture. On occasions, therefore, when Dengei proposed to pay one of these visits, he sent a warning to the doctor, who in his turn promptly apprised the people. It then became obviously necessary that the neighbours should inundate the doctor with presents of mats, pillows, tobacco, grog, &c., so that the god should be pleased with his visit. The house was then left to the doctor, the people getting away to the farthest end of the town, so that Dengei might not have his sight polluted with their unworthiness. The poor folks were always greatly relieved in the morning when they were told that the god had enjoyed the grog immensely and greatly appreciated the presents.

Among the young people of Fiji, of course, Christianity is now universal. I have yet ringing in my ears the first ' Meké-Meké na Lotu ' (Christian song) I heard in Levuka. A party of girls were singing for the edification of some tourists.

'O let im pe shai-pull,
  Shai-pull, shai-pull, shai-pull,
O let im pe shai-pull,
  Wen we pa to meed no mo.'

THE BOUNTY MUTINEERS

THE story of the mutineers of the ' Bounty ' and their strange adventures in the South Pacific has always had a peculiar fascination for English readers. Those who have read the case fully have freely justified the malcontents in their insubordination, particularly as the notorious Captain Bligh's subsequent behaviour when he was Governor of New South Wales amply showed what manner of man he was, and how easily he could make trouble among those about him who happened to have the misfortune to be serving under him. It has been placed beyond doubt that Captain Bligh treated the crew of the ' Bounty ' so badly during the voyage across the Pacific that the men were absolutely forced either to get rid of him by the plan which they adopted or by killing him outright.

The mutiny of the 'Bounty' took place in the year 1789. Bligh had made matters so uncomfortable for his crew that they at last resolved to rid themselves of him. Accordingly, after some parleying and desultory fighting between the Captain's party—which consisted of Bligh and a small portion of the crew who stood by him—and the mutineers, Bligh and his companions were placed in a boat, supplied with provisions, and set adrift upon the open sea. From the south-eastern Pacific, somewhere between Pitcairn Island and the Society's, the Captain with his little party of faithful comrades pushed on across the wide expanse of ocean, amongst the numerous fairy archipelagos, till they eventually landed in the neighbourhood of Java, in the East Indies. They were, of course, many months on the voyage, and it was many months more before they succeeded in reaching England.

In the meantime the mutineers started off upon a voyage of discovery on their own account. They touched at many places, but eventually made up their minds for a sojourn at Tahiti. Here they were hospitably treated by the natives, who, it will be remembered, earned the title of the Society Islands for their group through their sociable and agreeable characteristics. The ladies especially made themselves agreeable to the mutineers, who eventually selected Tahitian wives for themselves. Tahiti, or the Society's, has been justly called 'the Paradise of the Pacific.' The main island—Tahiti— is indeed lovely to look upon. Its fertility and verdure are not to be surpassed, even in the ocean of pearls. Although it is just a hundred years since the ' Bounty ' people were here, many relics of their residence in the group yet remain. But they stayed but a few years. Disturbances and disagreements having arisen among themselves, and also between them and the Tahitians, they

F

resolved upon seeking fresh fields and pastures new. A few of the malcontents of their number were left behind, while the remainder again started out upon the ocean. This time they hit upon Pitcairn Island as a landing place, and they resolved so firmly to make this their permanent home that they destroyed the vessel in which they came.

In the meantime Captain Bligh had reached England and reported the mutiny to the authorities. Action was immediately taken, as Bligh of course only represented his side of the tale, and the whole country universally sympathised with . him. The 'Pandora' was sent out to the Pacific to investigate the matter, and she returned to England a few years afterwards with a lot of the mutineers aboard. They were tried, and three of them hung up to the yard-arm for their complicity in the affair. The balance of these people, who had been left in the Pacific, clung together on Pitcairn Island, and developed in time into a considerable settlement. John Adams, one of the originals, died in the year 1829 at the age of fifty-six years. Adams had grown to be a kind of father to the people, who profited greatly by his teaching and example. He had retained his Bible amongst his effects, and had thus been enabled to keep Christianity alive in his flock. The mutineers, or rather their descendants, were eventually, in the year 1857, removed from Pitcairn Island to Norfolk Island. Norfolk Island will be remembered as one of the last of our English convict settlements in that part of the world. It became notorious through the severity and cruelty which characterised the treatment of the unfortunate convicts who were transported there many years ago. The late Marcus Clarke the Australian novelist, has given, in his well-known work, 'His Natural Life,' a graphic and terrible description of the horrors of Norfolk Island in the convict days. One looks upon the island now and forgets the

horrible in the contemplation of the lovely
spot. Norfolk Island stands a thousand
miles to the eastward of Sydney, about mid-
way, and in a line, between New Zealand
and New Caledonia. It consists of a series
of hills, crowned with magnificent groves of
gigantic pine, graceful palmetto, guava,
lemon, and fern trees. Yellow cornfields
wave by the side of gardens in which grow
the delicate cinnamon tree, the tea and
coffee shrubs, the sugar-cane, the banana,
and luxuriant vines.

The old barrack walls and stockades near
the landing place are the only things which
now remain to remind the traveller of the
gruesome old times. The settlers upon the
island now are under the care of the Rev.
Mr. Nobbs, a gentleman who has a great
deal to be proud of in the results which have
followed from his noble work amongst them.
Hard work, instruction, and amusement are
all equally attended to, and one is forcibly
struck with the advanced results which have

been attained in each of these departments. The island may be said to be one extensive and rich plantation. The scholarly attainments of the mass of the people reflect the highest credit upon the teachers. The avidity with which the younger section of the population follow up the ordinary national British sports is not to be surpassed by the proverbial keenness of the Australians in this respect. Tennis-courts abound. A team of cricketers is always ready to meet and defeat any visitors in that popular sport. A match is often played with visiting missionary teams from other islands and New Zealand, and, if my memory serves me rightly, the Norfolk Islanders have up to now an unbeaten record.

For some years after the mutiny of the ' Bounty ' the sympathy created by the hardships endured by Captain Bligh on his return voyage to England brought him into general favour, and little or no suspicion was directed towards him as a possible cause of the

trouble. It was after his appointment to the
Governorship of New South Wales, or Botany
Bay, as it was then called, that the real
character of the man made itself apparent.
He exercised the most arbitrary and unjust
conduct in the discharge of his duties as
Governor, and soon had the people of
Sydney bordering upon a state of revolution.
In fact, what was at one time called a serious
rebellion did break out, headed by the well-
known Captain Johnstone, of Annandale, a
member of the governing Council in Sydney
at the time. Captain Johnstone called out a
large section of the military, who were prepared to follow him, and they blockaded the
Governor in Government House. Bligh
became greatly terrified at the turn which
things had taken, and when Johnstone
eventually forced an entrance into Government House they found His Excellency
ignominiously concealed beneath the bed in
his bedroom. He was placed under arrest
by Captain Johnstone, who assumed for a

time, with the consent of the majority of the
Council and the people of Sydney, the
direction of the affairs of the Colony. Com-
munications were made to the home authorities, and the Governor's conduct fully
reported, with the result that the 'rebels'
were held justified in their conduct, and
Bligh was removed from his position.
Captain Johnstone, the hero of the rebellion,
lived in Sydney to a venerable old age,
having only died a few years since. He
was a popular 'old identity' figure in the
streets of Sydney, and died universally
lamented. Bligh was one of the few un-
popular Governors who have been sent to
Australia. He was the only really bad
ruler the New South Wales people have
had.

The descendants of the 'Bounty' mutineers
are a handsome people. There are probably
no prettier women in the world than the
women of Tahiti, and the Norfolk Islanders
owe much of the grace of their complexion

to their foremothers.   Some of the names
they adopt are quaint.   Thursday October
Christian, a son of Christian—one of the
mutineers—was one of their leading characters.   He has a large number of descendants
on the island, and the consequence is that
there are a goodly number of Thursdays and
Octobers knocking about.   A handsome
quadroon-looking youth called Oc'—an ab-
breviation of October—was the demon
bowler of the young colony when I visited
the island.

NA LAIRO

I HAVE seen in many of the fish shop windows in London a large kind of sea-crab which, dead, has reminded me in many respects of a dead lairo. I should like, however, to see him in his live state, to see if he conducts himself in the same manner as my affectionate acquaintance, the lairo of Fiji. I say my affectionate acquaintance, and I use the adjective advisedly. For who that has had any experience of the lairo will deny him an extraordinary proclivity for clinging to the human form divine? You can't make much out of the expression of his features, and some pessimists will say that he clings with felonious intent, but I can never feel justified in imputing vicious motives to a fellow-member of the natural world when I am not

sure but that he means well. Let us not be
too severe in our strictures. I have often
seen the lairo, like the tender-hearted dog
which licks the hand that smites it, turn with
a dogged persistence and endeavour to
embrace—and warmly, and possibly affection-
ately, embrace—the great toe of a foot which
has spurned it. And, if the physical capaci-
ties of the lairo will not admit of its embrac-
ing the object of its regard in the orthodox
way, round the waist, does not the little
animal display some sagacity in trying to hug
a portion of the human form which it can
hug comfortably and completely? It has a
partiality for the great toe, and it also may
be said to dearly like the thumb or finger.

I remember once reading a story of a
young woman in some part of America who
was wooed by a young farm-hand in her
neighbourhood. He was well up in farming,
but in love-making business he couldn't count
for much. He spent long evenings with the
girl, and would sit for hours with his arm

round her waist ; but speak to her, or indulge
in a conversation of any kind, he could not.
The painful monotony annoyed her, and lost
him his girl. 'She slung him,' as they
roughly say over that way.

It is just something of the same kind
which prompts the average man to a desire
to 'sling' a lairo when that affectionate animal
has taken a finger or a toe in its warm
embrace. The lairo says nothing—does not
even wink—when he is absorbed in business
of that kind ; but he just hangs on. And the
thing gets monotonous to the other party.
It thus happens that the lairo often gets
'slung,' and in a literal, not an allegorical,
sense. I have seen wicked men return the
embraces of a poor lairo by slinging him
forty yards or more, and not paying much
attention to the kind of place they were
slinging him to either.

I have had some experiences of the grasp
of the interesting creature. For every one
occasion, however, on which I have been

successfully embraced I dare say there are twenty or more occasions upon which I have persistently declined the friendly overtures made to me. I was once travelling along the coast of Goro, the large and fertile island in the centre of the Fiji group. Coming to a friend's house, I walked in at the open door, to find no one at home. The rule in Fiji in such a case is to help yourself to anything you want. I saw a sugar-bag in a corner, half full of something, probably yaqona root, as it is generally kept in such bags. I sent my servant for a bucket of water, while I strode across the room and picked up the bag, with a view of extracting a handful of grog. But what powerful grog I found it to be! What a strength it had! Two pieces of it seemed to come together suddenly and grip my finger through the bag with the grip of a vice. When my boy returned he found me dancing a most extraordinary kind of meké-meké on my own account, with the bag suspended to my finger. For the error of

one of their number, however, that small
community of lairos suffered. They might
have lived till dinner time in the planter's
house had it not been for the misplaced
affection of the erring one who caught hold
of my finger.

Scientifically, I am unable, through my
want of knowledge, to say much about the
lairo. I believe, however, that he belongs to
the order reptilia, and I know that in his
general habits he is amphibious. In size,
his usual average would be about as big as
a Fijian's head, and he is about as hard on
the outside. In fact, I think that if you
started firing alternate revolver shots at a
Fijian's head and a lairo, you would waste
about the same amount of lead upon each
before you succeeded in driving a hole in.
When the lairo is living ashore he digs holes
in the ground for his habitation, which he
seems to take a pride in furnishing upon the
latest improved principles. If you leave
your boots outside the door at night. and a

lairo comes along, he doesn't stop to inquire whether you may have any further use for them. He assumes that you have done with them, or you wouldn't leave them outside, in a lairo country, without a small chain or strong cord fastening them to the fence or wall. He takes them down his hole straight-way. They may not be much use to him—in fact, he couldn't get them on if he tried, but they help to fill up ; and, besides, they are, generally speaking, imported goods. The lairo thinks as much of imported goods as does an Australian native.

I went to the trouble of digging out an old man lairo once. I wanted to have an interview with him. I was prepared for a stormy interview ; in fact, made up my mind that that was the kind of interview which I must have with him. I didn't want any civility, any hand-shaking, or softness of that sort. I desired to see him more particularly with reference to a penknife, a hair brush, and several other articles which had dis-

appeared from the verandah one night.
These articles all came to the surface by
degrees as we excavated. We were also
surprised to find many other articles which
had not been particularly missed—old boots,
spoons, crockery ware, &c. The old man
had made a good all-round collection. When
we eventually got the proprietor of the
show to the surface a fierce battle commenced between him and my boy Tiemi
(Jimmy). Tiemi thirsted for blood, and I was
unable to save the lairo from a violent
death. I should like to have saved him, too ;
but I think if he remained on the place Tiemi
would have in any case assassinated him, or
left my service. The latter would have been
a painful alternative to both of us. Tiemi
hails from Mallicollo, in the Hebrides. His
case always reminds me of the lines written
by the notorious pickpocket Barrington, who
was transported to Botany Bay in the latter
years of last century. A play was performed
in Sydney in 1796 by a company of convicts,

and a prologue was written for the occasion
by Barrington.

> From distant climes, o'er widespread seas, we come,
> Though not with much éclat or beat of drum.
> True patriots we, for, be it understood,
> We left our country for our country's good.
> No private ends disgraced our generous zeal—
> What urged our travels was our country's weal ;
> And none will doubt but that our emigration
> Has proved most useful to the British nation.

Tiemi had also left Mallicollo for Mallicollo's good. Like Barrington, Tiemi had
broken the law of his country ; but he did
not want to undergo the disagreeable form of
a trial. He left suddenly on his own account.
They don't transport people from Mallicollo
—they possess no mundane Botany Bay to
which to transmit offenders. When you
commit a fairly serious offence there they
transport you without much delay to the
happy banana groves. Tiemi's offence
had consisted in the slaughter—in error, he
always maintains—of a pig belonging to the
Royal household. The law clearly sets forth
in Mallicollo that he who interferes with a

pig belonging to Royalty shall surely die, and
die of a sudden, too. Tiemi preferred to die
of consumption, or some other lingering complaint, in a foreign country.

The natives of Vanua Levu and other
islands have a curious way of catching the lairo.
The crab has a great propensity for climbing
up the coco-nut trees and pulling down
the young fruit, which he breaks open and
eats when he comes down again. Where the
lairos are numerous it can be easily seen that
the coco-nut plantations have a poor chance
of success, and so the natives have adopted
an ingenious way of thinning out the crabs.
The lairo generally goes up the tree early in
the night, that is to say, between dusk and
midnight, and he remains pottering about a
good while, generally coming down as the
day begins to break. The plan is for the
natives to go round after midnight and tie
great wisps of grass round the coco-nut trees
about ten feet from the ground. Then, as
the lairo comes down—backwards of course,

G

as this is his only way of descending—and reaches the tuft of grass, fancying he is once more on *terra firma*, he lets go his hold on the tree and comes tumbling to the ground a mangled mass. Where the crabs have been numerous I have often seen small schooner-loads of them lying round the foot of each coco-nut tree in the morning. When the lairo season is at its full the natives have terrific feasts ; in fact, there are thousands of them left over for export, if only the trade in that class of edible had been developed.

The life of the lairo would be fairly enjoy-able were it not for the annoyance to which he is subjected by the small boy tribe. Boys have not yet learnt to use the pea-shooter or the shanghai in Fiji. They play cricket to a limited degree only. This is chiefly owing to the fact that an umpire is a necessity to control the play. Then the umpire generally gets half killed before the innings is over. An accident policy on a Fijian umpire's life would be a very bad risk

for an insurance office. Hence the small
boy, generally speaking, devotes his recreation
hours to annoying the lairo. In fact, trapping
the lairo, or persecuting him, is a kind of
instinct with the boy. As the young cat
knows what to do when she sees her first
mouse, so does the Fiji boy, as soon as he
begins to toddle, by a species of instinct,
stand around a good deal where lairos most
do congregate, armed to the teeth with junks
of rock and other implements of destruction.
One of the funniest physical features of the
lairo is the construction of his eyes. In a
full-grown crab the eye is about an inch long
when fully projected ; or, rather, the eye is
fixed at the end of a projecting arm about an
inch long. This arm is projected or with-
drawn at will, of course. When the lairo
wants to look down the road he doesn't get
up on his hind legs or climb on a fence to do
it ; he merely throws up his eyes. When he
wants to wink he has to draw them in again
temporarily.

Lairo hunting is one of the popular sports of the Fijian people. He is always hunted at night time, with torches. The light dazzles him, and he falls an easy prey. A *koro*, or town, generally turns out *en masse* when the proper hunting season is on. Young people generally take a lively interest in the sport, and the dark character of an *uvi* jungle will always commend it as a desirable spot for a little flirting. You have often heard it said that love is blind. I don't know what to think of that favourite saying when I remember things which I have seen in Fiji. I have known some marvellous cases of long-sightedness, in fact, which would to some extent explode the blind theory. I have known a pair of lovers to find each other on occasions when the darkness of the night has been such that old experienced people have not been able to see through it.

The lairo is a favourite dish with the Fijian. A prominent trait in the Fijian character—his tender-heartedness and regard for the feelings of other creatures—is a strange feature to find in the constitution of a people who were, up to a few years ago, to be ranked amongst the most thorough-paced cannibals on the face of the earth. The captured lairo is put out of his misery in a merciful way. A thin, well-sharpened hardwood stick, somewhat resembling a bodkin, is used to settle him. The point of the stick is dexterously driven into him at a point immediately under his left armpit. It probably strikes him somewhere in the region of the heart, for he dies immediately.

If the Fijian recognises in the lairo a delicacy, the lairo, in his own turn, when in the land of the quick, has many partialities in the matter of delicacies himself. He is fond of ' medicine ' for one thing. I was travelling in company with a Fijian once. He carried a basket of which he appeared to be very careful ; there was evidently some live stock in it. I asked him what it was. ' Medicine ' was the prompt reply. The medicine turned out to be a brace of chickens. This is the kind of health restorer which is most appreciated by the lairo. He will travel a long way out of his track to surround a chicken. The proverbial American chicken-stealer is not a better hand at skinning a barnyard of chicks than the lairo. The roost, however, is the only thing which defies him. But the nigger has had to drop the roost-raiding business of late years since the Americans patented the *torpedo* chicken!

THE EUROPEAN PIONEER
OF FIJI

ONE of the most interesting characters in the
latter-day history of the Pacific was Charlie
Savage, a resourceful Cockney, who found
his way into the Fiji group as cabin-boy on
board a trading ship which sailed from the
Thames in the early days of the present
century. The vessel in question, having got
in among the Fiji Islands, was cast away on
the coral reef at Nairai, a little island lying
to the eastward of Ovalau. The natives of
Nairai pounced upon the prize with avidity,
and all hands on board the vessel, with the
exception of Charlie Savage, were in due
course got ready for the oven and eaten by
the Nairaians. Charlie Savage, owing doubt-
less to the fact that he was cabin-boy and had

a good run of the commissariat department, was in the pink of condition at the time, and as the Nairai people were bound to carry some part of their fortunate find to the ruling authorities at Bau by way of tribute, Charlie was kept for this purpose, and so escaped the general massacre. The bad weather which brought about the wreck of the vessel prevented the Nairai people from running their canoes down to Bau for a little time, and by degrees Charlie got to be on something like friendly terms with his captors. They had looted the vessel and carried off such things as they understood the use of, but among the neglected cargo was a quantity of gunpowder and some fire-arms. Securing these, the stranded Cockney amused himself, and greatly interested and excited the natives, by shooting birds and other things, and when, eventually, they took him on to Bau and made an offering of him to King Tanoa, the chief ruler of the Fiji archipelago, they had some wonderful tales to tell of Charlie's prowess with the *dakai* (fire-stick). So it came about that King Tanoa, having plenty of fresh meat when he wanted it, decided not to eat Charlie Savage, but to keep him and learn something of the wonderful 'fire-stick' which he had brought into the country. It was soon conveyed to Charlie that the King would like an exhibition of the use of the *dakai*, and the royal wish was promptly gratified. Birds, pigs, and even men were placed *hors de combat* under the royal wish, and it was not long before the King himself picked up the use of a gun. Tanoa was a crafty monarch, and quick to act when a new stroke of policy occurred to him, and as soon as he had mastered the use of the *dakai*, and grasped the effect of it, he sent a couple of messengers off at full speed across country to Na Droga to apprise the King of that place (who had, by the way, given Tanoa's land forces a severe drubbing a little while before) ' that he did not care a coco-nut for him, and that he was only a poor nigger after all.'

This insult stirred the King of Na Droga to a high pitch of wrath, and, without wasting any more time than it took to cook and eat the two messengers from Bau, the Na Droga fighting contingent was on the march to King Tanoa's country. Expecting them, Tanoa, with the help of Charlie Savage, had rigged up something in the shape of a rough fort at Bau, facing the coast of Viti-Levu, and when the Na Droga warriors appeared on the scene and came prancing across the shallow reef between the mainland and Bau they received a peppering from the little fort which surprised them not a little.

The Bau forces were completely victorious, and the news of the wonderful new weapon and its marvellous and destructive effects for fighting purposes soon spread from one end of the Fijian archipelago to the other. The King, accompanied by Charlie. Savage, now made trips to various parts of the group, and in a short time the whole of the islanders, from Rambi to Kandavu, from

the Yasawas to Loma Loma, rendered sub-
mission to the King of Bau. Old Tanoa;
in a proper spirit of gratitude, heaped honours
and rewards on Charlie Savage, who became
the owner of large plantation properties and
of a fine selection of beautiful wives as well.
This elevation from the poor condition of a
cook-boy on a trading vessel to that of a
large land-owner and sort of Prime Minister
and Commander-in-Chief in an important
kingdom tended somewhat to turn Charlie's
head, and some of the veracious chronicles of
the period point to him as having developed
into a very high-handed and overbearing
personage. From hammering his wives when
they disagreed with him up to shooting
Fijians who came inconveniently in his way,
Charlie Savage committed all sorts of criminal acts, and there was some relief felt generally when, in leading an expedition up the
Macuata coast on one occasion, he was
driven into a corner, his forces routed, and he
himself mbutirak'd to death.

If Charlie did but little good for himself in the end, he certainly did good things for Fiji, and particularly for King Tanoa, who was enabled by his help to confederate the various groups forming the Fijian archipelago into one united kingdom, so that when Cako-Bau succeeded his father on the throne at Bau he found himself at the head of one of the strongest powers in the South Pacific in those days.   In the first years of his rule Cako-Bau exceeded his father, and, indeed, exceeded his royal predecessors for many generations, in the brutality of his behaviour and the open encouragement he gave to cannibalism and other horrible vices of the period.   It is related of Cako-Bau that he killed his first man when only six years of age.   In one of the gruesome functions held in the royal compound on the island of Bau in those times a captured chief from the Raki Raki country was bound hand and foot, and the young prince, who was just able to lift a club, was put forward to kill the unfortunate *turaga*. It took him some time, according to all accounts, but he finished the task himself; so when hardly out of his infancy he was guilty of his first criminal act as a homicide. It is satisfactory to learn, however, that later on, mainly through the influence of his loyal friend the late King George of Tonga, King Cako-Bau received the *papalagi* missionaries at Bau, and eventually himself became a professing and very sincere Christian. In the latter years of his life he endeavoured in every possible way to atone for the ruffianism of his early days, and much sympathy was felt for him both among his own people and by the European residents of the group, who now began to increase largely in numbers. When the old King died—a few years after he ceded the islands to Great Britain, in 1874—there was general sorrow in the group, and the scene at his funeral on Bau was a most impressive one. A British man-of-war was sent to Bau for the occasion, and the then Governor of Fiji, Sir William des Vœux, officially attended on behalf of the Queen.

I remember once meeting on the Rewa River a granddaughter of Charlie Savage, a rather pretty octoroon girl, who showed considerable pride in the memory of her buccaneering progenitor. There are, I believe, many descendants of Savage's knocking about the Fijis. Some years ago there were found in the house of a chief in the Namosi Valley several articles of silver-ware that had evidently come from some of the Catholic churches on the Pacific slope of South America. They were known to have been in Savage's possession, and the conjecture was that the ship to which he belonged had been carrying off some loot in one of the war times from the South American coast when she foundered at Nairai.

AMONG THE MAORIS

WHAT a surprise that must have been for the Englishman who was one day strolling down Queen Street, Auckland. He espied the well and fashionably dressed figure of a young lady a short distance in front. Her head was concealed from his view by a sunshade of the most gaudy pattern. He became a deeply interested party at once. Young Englishmen out in the colonies for a holiday invariably take a keen interest in our fair sex, more especially when their personal appearance is attractive. And our girls very often possess fathers who own considerable stretches of 'jumbuck' property, which is an additional attraction.

The young fellow pushed ahead till he came on a level with the lady. Imagine his surprise, when he looked in her face, to find it copper-coloured, with a black clay pipe stuck leisurely in her mouth. His disenchantment was sudden and complete.

The American citizen is a great smoker as a rule ; in fact, the rule has come to be so generally recognised that the American now passes, with most people, as the tallest smoker in creation.

But the Maori can give him a long start. And the Maori would be prepared to bet on himself, too, I dare say. The proverbial keenness of the Yankee for speculation is as nothing when the Maori enters the arena.

The Maori, as a smoker, begins young. On my first visit to Auckland I saw a portrait in a photographer's window in which a mother was shown with a child slung, in the orthodox fashion, upon her back—the mother was represented smoking a large-bowled meerschaum, while the baby sucked at a diminutive Irish cuddy. My first impression, of course, was that this was meant to convey some artistic idea of the photographer's, and not a representation of things as they were. But I afterwards learned that children took kindly and early to the fragrant weed.

I was one evening the guest of a Maori *rangatira* in Whaka-rewa-rewa. The party was a small one—the Maori, his wife, his sister, and myself. We had a rubber at whist, and my host suggested an adjournment for refreshment and a smoke. While we were enjoying our weed a child—about three years of age, I should think—suddenly put in an appearance, and made a formal demand for a smoke.

'Finish my cigar,' said my host, tendering his butt. But the child would have none of him. It threw its head in mamma's lap, and made a disjointed request, throwing occasional side glances at the stranger, for mamma's *pipe*. My own experience has taught me that cigars give poor satisfaction to a real smoker. I therefore suppose that

H

the child had already learned what it had taken me years to gather.

I said to the mother on this occasion, ' Fine boy, that.' She laughed as she replied, ' Ko te Wahine ' (' It's a girl ').

The Maori is a born orator, according to the generally accepted notion. But he knows just exactly when to talk. Upon an occasion when speaking is required of him, he will speak practically, forensically, politically, or in any way which best suits the occasion. But when 'speech is silvern, silence golden,' no living creature can hold his tongue so smartly and so effectually as the Maori. A game of draw-poker in a Maori whare is a veritable quakers' meeting.

The Maori people have never taken kindly to the British. Although peace has reigned in the country for many years, the Maori preserves a sullenness which at times creates some alarm in the political atmosphere. The great King Country, a belt of rich but undeveloped country lying between the Wairarapa and the now celebrated Hot Lake district, has not been open to Europeans till quite a recent date. After many years of discussion the Government have at last succeeded in gaining the consent of the Maori people to the construction of a railway through the country. The first sod of the railway was turned at Te Awamutu, a few miles from the home of King Tawhiao at Whati-whati-hoe, some years ago. Wahanui, the Maori orator, and Parliamentary representative for one of the Maori districts, went to Te Awamutu with the then Premier, Sir Robert Stout. It had been arranged, of course, that the Premier should turn the first sod. Before the appointed hour for the ceremony, however, a *korero* was held, at which the Maoris decided that their member, Wahanui, should turn the sod, while the Premier was relegated to a back seat. Accordingly Wahanui was the principal performer at the ceremony, Sir Robert Stout being allowed the privilege of wheeling away the barrow which contained the sod.

The Maori has also, when compared with the other aboriginal inhabitants of the Pacific, been very slow to embrace Christianity. When I was in Tauranga once I was called upon at my hotel by a young Maori from the neighbouring native town of Judea. Before leaving he asked me to come and take dinner with him the following evening. I was on hand in due course, and after dinner we lit our pipes and had a stroll through the town. Passing a church—the only one in the town —I asked him, 'What religion have you got here?' 'Oh,' he replied, 'we have two here; some are Cathoricks' (the Maori never uses an L), 'and some b'long to the other chap.' 'Which chap?' I asked, 'Wesleyan or Church of England?' 'No,' he said, 'none of them. Oh, I dunno,' he continued, ' I never take any interest in these things, so I don't know which it is; anyway, there's a

lot about Solomon and Methuselah in it;
perhaps you know it.'

Tawhiao, the late Maori King, held
whatever social and political status he
possessed just as an English lord of poor
character retains his title and rank. Morally
he was bereft of power amongst the people.

Rewi—the hero of Orakau—Te Wheoro,
Taiaroa, and many others possessed large
influence.

But as regards illustrious descent,
Tawhiao was the Cecil, the Norfolk, of
Maoriland. His dynasty changed its ruling
name a generation before him—his official
title being Potatau the Second. His full
name was 'Matutaeru Te Puké-puké Te
Paue Tu Karato Te-a Potatau Te Whero-
whero Tawhiao,' or Potatau II., and he was
a direct descendant of the celebrated pioneer
Hotonui, who came in the great war canoe
Tainui, from Hawaiki, and settled in Kawhia,
seven or eight hundred years ago. Here is a
little of the genealogy. Tapaue was a dis-

tinguished descendant of Hotonui, who was followed by his son Tawhia, whose son was Tuata, whose son was Te Rauanganga, whose son was Te Whero-whero, whose son was Tawhiao, or Potatau II.

In his personal character Tawhiao had little regal dignity. He did unkingly things, and moved about generally in an unkingly way. When I was at Rangiriri some years ago Tawhiao met me and showed me over the old battle-field. This was the scene of the first collision between the Maoris and the British troops in the great Maori war. We visited the native town on the northern shore of Lake Whakaré. Coming back across Whakaré to Rangiriri the King took an oar in the canoe, and worked hard with it all the way, and the disgust of the other Maoris aboard was but ill-concealed.

The Maoris are keen business men, and many of them rank amongst the richest people in New Zealand. I was sitting in a friend's office in Christchurch one day when a Maori came in. He spoke to my friend for a few moments, handed him a cheque, and left again. When he had gone the cheque was shown to me. It was drawn for 10,000*l.* I said, 'That's a big figure for a Maori.' 'Oh,' said he, 'that's nothing ; that man is worth over half a million of money.' It was the late Hon. Mr. Taiaroa, for many years Parliamentary representative for the South Maori division, but later a member of the Upper House.

The Maori character of the century was Hongi-Hika, who was born in the year 1777. Hongi-Hika was 'hard of christening,' and the old people prophesied that he would be a bad man. The christening ceremony is a funny one. The candidate is got ready and a list of names produced. The first names on the list are those of good people, such as John, Joseph, Matthew, Luke, and so on. Further down you come upon the wicked ones —Nero, Guy Fawkes, Richard, and such. I once attended a christening near Ateamuri, where the tail end of the list contained the name of Wirimu Karatistoni (William Gladstone). The child is held up and the mother recites the names slowly, one after the other. The first move which the baby makes in the direction of a sneeze or a cry fixes its nomenclature. The name that he sneezes or cries upon belongs to him for ever. If he happens to take things coolly, and fails to take action before the mother gets down amongst the political and other odious names, his surrounding friends are stricken with sadness, as they know he will turn out a bad one. Such was Hongi-Hika. Hongi came to England in 1820, in company with Waikato. They were well received by George the Fourth, who gave Hongi a suit of armour and a lot of valuable presents in the shape of jewellery. When Hongi reached Sydney on his return he converted the jewellery into muskets, powder, and ball, and commenced to play Napoleon Bonaparte as soon as he landed in his own country, the Bay of

Islands.   He marched from north to south,
carrying death and destruction wherever he
went.   His name was, indeed, a terror in the
land.

The Maoris are a courageous and self-
possessed people.   But I have seen great
strong men shudder at the mention of the
word ' Hongi ! '

ROBINSON CRUSOE'S ISLAND

JUAN FERNANDEZ AND THE GALAPAGOS

I READ a paper not long since in which the writer endeavoured to show that the island upon which the original of Defoe's ' Robinson Crusoe' made his home was none other than Trinidad, the islet on the east coast of South America, about which we have lately been frightened by the Brazilians, who, after standing a good deal of 'John Bull' bounce, at last let the British Government know that if it did not abandon all claims to the island the Rio Republic would declare war on us. So we had to clear out, of course. But no arguing, however ingenious, can upset the well-established fact that Alexander Selkirk was cast adrift from his ship off the island of Juan

Fernandez, in the south-eastern Pacific Ocean, in the year 1706. He had quarrelled with his skipper, who got rid of him by driving him into a dingy and sending him ashore. All the accounts state, however, that he was humanely supplied with a quantity of provisions, a Bible, hatchet, gun, and other trifles of sporting gear likely to prove useful to a man who was about to take up his residence on a lonely island for an indefinite period. He does not appear, however, to have had a bottle of patent medicine amongst his effects, which has always been a matter of surprise to me. The papers in the colonies are constantly giving us long accounts of how Chinese Gordon went to Khartoum armed with nothing but his Bible and a small bag containing a few clothes and a bottle of one of the much advertised articles. They also often tell us that George Washington, Oliver Cromwell, and other distinguished but long-defunct individuals invariably carried bottles of these useful cures. That Selkirk had none there is hardly any doubt. The skipper, in all probability, had none aboard. He was an illiterate man very likely—couldn't read, and therefore had never read about them.

I have an old acquaintance in Fiji who is rather short-sighted. He is fond of reading, however, and subscribes to many papers. Amongst other amiable qualities he is possessed of a good·temper. He is only ruffled once in a way. This happens upon occasions when a newspaper has 'got at him,' as he terms it. I called upon him one day, and the atmosphere in his immediate presence appeared to be charged with electricity generated of the language he had been using. He pointed to a newspaper and hoarsely requested me to 'look at that.' 'That' was an attractively headed paragraph, ' Hints for intending coffee-planters in Fiji.' Half a column was devoted to an elaborate dissertation upon coffee culture ; the planter was advised to use this thing and that, but he was solemnly warned that he would go to the dogs

altogether if he failed to keep on hand a good
supply of some quack nostrum or other.

Alexander Selkirk spent four years and
four months upon the island of Juan
Fernandez, when he was picked up by a
passing vessel and brought to England, which
place he reached in the year 1711.

His look-out station, where he probably
spent most of his time looking out to sea in
the hope of catching sight of a passing ship,
still exists upon the island, and there are
many other spots which are supposed to show
traces of his occupation.

It was Mr. Cowper who said, I think,
that Alexander Selkirk was monarch of all
he surveyed. This particular Alexander
was probably the most unhappy monarch
who ever reigned. Even with plenty of
company, and a good supply of the necessaries of life, the ruler of Juan Fernandez
would have but a poor time of it.

There is a man on the island now—a
Chilian—who rents it from the Chilian

Government for a few hundred dollars a
year. The island itself is of little or no use
to him; but there is a guano reef in the
neighbourhood, which brings him a good
revenue. The Chilian has a wife, who con-
tributes in a great measure to break the
monotony of his existence upon the place.
She does not always confine her efforts in
the breaking line to the monotony either.
He wishes that she did. She very nearly
broke his head on one occasion when I was
there. He told me confidentially, over a
glass in my cabin a few days after, that he
would give her 'what Murphy gave his
missus' some day, if she didn't alter her
ways.

You do not know, perhaps, what Murphy
gave his missus? The expression is in
popular use on the western coast of South
America, and thereby hangs a tale. The
Republic of Ecuador is one of the most
interesting States in this part of the world.
The equator runs through the capital city,

Quito. The Galapagos, a group of islands
lying out in the ocean to the west of
Ecuador, belong to that State, and are made
use of as a convict settlement. A convict is
brought over from Atacames, or Guayaquil,
deposited on the Galapagos, and left to look
after himself, the ship which brought him
returning to Ecuador. The term of his
penal servitude for life invariably expires
upon the arrival of the next vessel. Whalers
are constantly calling in here for a supply of
beef—several of the islands are overrun with
cattle, and a captain is always ready to take
a man away when he is willing to work his
passage. Señor Murfé, who was a descendant
of an ancient family of the name of Murphy,
which originally emigrated from Flanders
and settled in Ireland, was for many years
the keeper of a gin saloon in the city of
Quito. The Señor was gay and festive in
his personal habits, and, as often happens to
people of this temperament, he had con-
tracted an unfortunate matrimonial alliance.

The Señor's wife developed a dangerous habit of entering the gin saloon and smiting him about the head with a bottle. In size they were disproportionately matched. The Señor was a little man, while his better half was a big woman. He couldn't safely resort to the old-fashioned system of hammering her. He was sorely perplexed for a long time, and was one day pouring his troubles into the sympathetic ear of an old acquaintance. The friend suggested that the Señor should melt a drop of lead in her ear some night. Here was a neat plan ready to hand. It was a novel method of killing a person, even in South America. In due course, one morning the unfortunate woman was found dead in her bed. Many men out that way have since given their wives 'what Murphy gave his missus.'

You will be wondering how the Señor got on, though. They do not let a man off in Ecuador, as they do in other parts of America, for murdering a wife. He was

tried, convicted, and sentenced to transporta-
tion to the Galapagos for life.   This was a
heavy sentence, but the Señor had voted
against the judge who tried him at the last
election, and he now reaped the reward of
his perfidy.   Murfé had money, and before
he was transported he arranged that a small
schooner should be at once sent out to the
islands to bring him back again.   Accordingly the Government vessel conveyed him
to the Galapagos and landed him.   A few
hours later he stepped aboard his schooner'
and started on his way back.   The schooner
was a clipper, and she reached Atacames
before the other vessel.

Murfé is a great character over that way.
We went round to his saloon one night when
we were up in Quito and had a chat with
him.   We had heard of his escapade, and
broached the subject.   He was quite proud
of the manner in which he had managed the
affair.   I couldn't help asking him, though,
how it was they didn't bring him up again

I

when he came back. ' Don't you know it's a rule all over the wur-rld,' said the Señor, ' nivir to thry a man twoice for a criminal offince ? ' That was a settler. How can one argue against logic like that, especially when it is accompanied by the persuasiveness of an Irishman ? The Señor, though a citizen of Ecuador, retains in a marked degree the personal characteristics which distinguished his ancestors.

How devoutly the average boy pictures to himself as he reads the life of Robinson Crusoe the pleasures of such a life. How devoutly he wishes he could be cast away upon some lonely island, with a gun, and a cat, and a dog, and lots of other *impedimenta*, so that he might act Robinson Crusoe. I know that I used to feel that way a good deal when I was a boy. I have since had the distinction of acting the *rôle* of Robinson Crusoe for a short season, and I have no particular desire to do it again. I was thrown away once in the Carolines, and managed to pick my way through reefs and drifts to the shores of a small island. It was a much more hospitable island than Juan Fernandez, as coco-nuts grew in large quantities all over it. I spent the first ten days in frightful misery, more through the want of company than anything else. The most pleasant day I had was that following a night upon which I had been troubled a good deal with dreams. The subject of my dreams was something novel to think about. The loneliness of a man's situation is something intense when he is compelled to fall back on his dreams for fresh matter. I had begun to think that I was also monarch of all I surveyed. This idea of mine was rudely dispelled one day. A huge native approached me, with what I imagined at first to be friendly gestures. I had got him to throw down his spear by throwing down a piece of bamboo, and signing to him to follow my example. He came up close, and I commenced to try my languages on him. All of a sudden he

made a violent kick at me, which would have
left me powerless in his hands if it had not
been for the greatest luck in the world. We
then fought for our lives, as it were. There
is a universal rule to be followed in fighting
a Polynesian. If you hit him about the head
you smash your knuckles, and you only
amuse him ; you do not hurt him. But his
binjie, as the Australian blacks call it, is his
weak spot. As Artemus Ward would have
put it, my new acquaintance struck me a
violent blow on the left fist with his stomach,
after which he sat down to have a spell. I
promptly handcuffed him with my belt, and
kept him in charge till next day. I had some
trouble with more of his tribe before I succeeded in getting away to the next island,
-and eventually from the group. But I want
no more experiences in the Robinson Crusoe
line.

NEW CALEDONIA AND ITS CONVICTS

As the reader will probably know, New Caledonia is a French colony, and has been used by the French Government for many years as a penal settlement.

The island of New Caledonia is about 300 miles in length by an average breadth of 40 miles. It lies about 950 miles north-east from Sydney, and runs in a south-easterly and north-westerly direction between latitude 20 and 23 degrees south.

Entering the roadstead of Noumea, the first impression which one gets of the physical character of the country is not very inviting. Great arid-looking mountain ridges stretch away behind the town, and the further knowledge of the country which one gains upon an extended acquaintance with it only tends to confirm the first impressions formed of its barrenness. There are, of course, many fertile spots to be found upon New Caledonia. The banks of the rivers have all been selected at different times by cattle-raisers and planters. Noumea is situated upon a kind of flat, on the shore of a most picturesque harbour. The harbour itself is very secure, being almost land-bound, as it has Ile Nou situated directly in its mouth. Ile Nou is, of course, the first spot of interest which attracts the traveller as the vessel passes close under its shore. This is the chief penal dépôt in the colony, about 8,000 convicts being confined upon it. They are conveyed from Ile Nou every morning in barges to the mainland to enter upon their daily hard labour.

Noumea would appear to have had its creation about forty years ago, when the Crimean War was going on. Thus we find the main thoroughfare called Alma Street.

There is also Inkerman Street, the Hôtel Sébastopol, and so on.

Many of the public buildings in Noumea present a rather imposing appearance from the harbour. There are several military barracks of huge dimensions, and the hospital on the northern side of the town holds a commanding position. Many of the wealthier residents have their picturesque-looking private residences dotted over the sides of the hills at the rear of the town.

Noumea is very cosmopolitan in the constitution of its inhabitants. The French element, of course, predominates, but other nationalities are represented. The Celt blooms in great profusion. ' Who goes there? queried a sentry once as some people were passing him in the dark. ' Uz, Frinch,' was the reply.

The great social lever in Noumea is Freemasonry. It would be unjust to recklessly credit this popular and deserving institution with any hand in ways that are dark, but it is certain that in this part of the world rumour attributes to the craft a rather un-enviable connection with the escape of con-victs from the settlement. The escape of Henri Rochefort, Pascal Grousset, and Oliver Pain in the ' P. C. E.' some years ago is pointed to as a triumph of the fraternity in the matter of standing by a brother. This case, however, could fairly be looked upon as a political one. The trouble arises where the agent appears upon the scene, prepared, upon receiving a fee of 50 or 100 francs, to work the lever, and hoist the cut-throat or the forger upon the already over-burdened populations of Sydney and Brisbane.

Touching the Rochefort affair, the man who took a leading part in the preparations for that escapade was practically ruined through it. He had been carrying on a lucra-tive business as an hotel-keeper in Noumea, and his connection with the affair led to the confiscation of his property and his banish-ment from the colony. He afterwards kept a small hotel in Sydney, but never did well, and has always been appealing to Rochefort for help.

I was a lad at the time of the terrible Franco-German war. Mayne Reid and Fenimore Cooper supplied us in the main with our spiritual food in those days. But these graphic hero painters fell out of demand at the time when newspapers were full of the exploits of Gustave Flourens and Aurelles du Paladin. And what noble pictures we had in our minds of the persons of Henri Roche-fort and his companions. A soldier and an orator, a proper conventional six-footer, with the conventional moustache—who of us would not have hypothecated his pocket-money for a whole year to go and look upon the exiled hero of the Commune? I shall never forget the thrilling interest with which we heard the news of the arrival of Rochefort with his companions at Newcastle. They remained but a few days in the district before they started off on their way to London. I remember one morning passing in front of the hotel at which they were staying. Fortune favoured me. As I passed, the party of political *évadés* walked out of an upstair room on to the balcony. I rooted myself to the spot to realise the scene properly. They had some of the mortal element about them, though, after all. They smoked. But what would I not have given to be able to roll a cigarette *à la Rochefort*. I was only learning to smoke at the time.

What a pity it is that time and experience knock so much of the fine edge off our ideas of admiration for the great. During late years it has been my fortune to have considerable communion with tribunes of the people, with princes, and even with kings. The result is that I would not walk a hundred yards now to see a hero or a monarch.

Talking of my connection with Royalty, I was once acting as Prime Minister and Commander-in-Chief of the Forces to a South Sea potentate. The kingdom was twenty-two miles long by about two miles in breadth. But the King had established a protectorate over some neighbouring islets. The *protectorate* part of the business was a grand feature in the administration of the affairs of the kingdom. Before I had taken office the King encountered some trouble from the people on the islets, who, in their foolish way, protested that they wanted no protection whatever. His Majesty's method of protecting them did not fit in with their ideas of political economy. He collected all their coco-nuts for them, converted the nuts into copra, and sold it to white traders, keeping the money for his own personal use. After I had been in office for a few days I tried to induce the old man to go halves with them, but he couldn't see his way to do it. The army had to be kept up. The army always wanted something. There were about 47 men in it altogether, and only a short time previously the King had bought a pair of trousers for one of the ovisas. The ovisa had not worn them a day when the whole army clamoured for trousers. In fact, a mutiny seemed to be at hand; the men were growing impatient and impudent, and one had actually the effrontery to tell His Majesty that if he were not supplied with a *red shirt* he would 'bust up' the whole business. The old man was troubled, and he determined to hold all the money he could get for the purpose of conciliating the army. So that the protectorate over the islets went on as before.

We had a curious method of drilling in the army. The first occasion upon which I took charge I began to use some orders which I had formulated for the purpose. I gave the order, *Mata totonu* (eyes straight, or eyes front). An ovisa came over to me. 'Oh,' he said, 'never mind that; we just give them *Shouldah hums!* for everything, and they imitate or follow us in what we require them to do.' I had to fall in with the arrangement, and accordingly, to the order

' shouldah hums' every movement was done.
Right wheel, left wheel, stand-at-ease, and
all, were performed with alacrity to the order,
Shouldah hums!

I went along very well as Premier till the
King and I disagreed.   He annexed my
watch, and I wanted it back again.   I had to
threaten to blow a hole into him with a Lancaster ' R.I.C.,' which I always carried, before
he would disgorge, but he retaliated by invest-
ing me with the ancient order of the sack.

The traveller to Noumea naturally betakes
himself to Ile Nou in search of the interesting.   During one of my visits to the island I
had a conversation with the notorious Parisian
assassin Abadie.   A young friend of mine
from the Mauritius, who accompanied me,
took great interest in the arch-assassin, as
he was living in Paris at the time of Abadie's
capture and conviction, and had, in fact,
strangely enough, given evidence at the trial.
My friend lived with his uncle in Paris, and
one evening had occasion to step across the

street to purchase a newspaper.   Returning, he was hardly well inside when a commotion at the door attracted his attention.   He rushed out to find a man weltering in his blood near the doorstep.   He was just in time to catch a glimpse of the murderer as he hastened away.   He had time to take a longer look at the assassin when he confronted him in a court of justice to assist in his prosecution.   But he had time to survey him more leisurely still as the three of us stood chatting together on Ile Nou.   Abadie had been the director of a gang of assassins in Paris.   As my friend offered him a cigarette he put the question, ' I wonder how it would have been if I had crossed the street a minute earlier, just as you had come up with that fellow?' ' You would never have been here,' was the convict's reply.

Another interesting character here is the worthy who gave himself out as a Roman Catholic bishop and collected immense sums of money in different parts of France for convent building purposes.   Like most swindlers, he did not know where to stop, and he is now booked for the rest of his natural life for a residence in New Caledonia.

The convict band is also a striking feature in connection with Ile Nou.   This band, which is about the finest I have ever heard, plays for five hours on Thursdays and Sundays in the public park in the centre of Noumea.   During the remainder of the week they devote five hours a day to practice, so that they ought to play well.   I should almost be inclined to think that this continued application to music would tend to make the performers stale.   But, after all, who would not sooner beat a drum all day than break stones along the roadside?   I am sure, if I were compelled to choose between the two, I should elect to have the music, even if I had to blow the trombone.

There is a strange character who moves majestically up and down the streets of Noumea, whose dress and general appearance catch the stranger's eye at once.   This is an Algerian sheik, who was transported to Noumea after the rebellion in Algiers which followed the rising of the Commune in Paris. The sheik was one of the leaders of the revolt, and when the rebellion was crushed he, with some companions, was sentenced to death for his complicity in the trouble.   But during Marshal MacMahon's time in Algeria, many years before, the young Algerian chief was a loyal subject and a close personal friend and ally of MacMahon's.   When the sheik got into trouble the Marshal had just been elected President of the Republic.   The sheik's mother hastened to Paris, appealed to the President, and saved her son's life. The alternative was given him of banishment to New Caledonia.   The old man is very popular.   He walks round the streets on parole, and is allowed the privilege of adoring his own God in his own way.

KANAKAS AND 'KAI-OUI-OUIS'

THE antithesis of the desert, with its green and refreshing oasis, is to be found on the bosom of the Pacific Ocean, some five hundred miles to the north-east of Brisbane, the capital of Queensland. As one sails over the calm face of the ocean, fanned by the gentle breezes for which the Pacific is remarkable, it is with a feeling somewhat akin to pain and abhorrence that one approaches the desolate-looking shores of New Caledonia. The smoke from the dreaded bush fires is seen rising from amongst the forests of *niaouli* along the sides of the mountain ridges, and the imagination can depict the comforts enjoyed by the unhappy *libéré*, whom the Government of the Republic has so thoughtfully furnished with a free land grant of

K

thirty-six acres in the scrubby forests among the mountain gorges.

When the traveller to New Caledonia passes through the narrow straits which divide Ile Nou from the southern headland of the harbour of Noumea, he bids good-bye to the sweet Pacific breezes till he emerges through the straits again. For heat, and mugginess, and general 'cussedness' in the matter of climate, the town of Noumea is almost equal to Cooktown, Queensland, which spot is far and away the warmest corner on the warm continent of Australia. The heat of Cooktown greatly assists the preachers of the Gospel up that way. When people experience the heat of that place, and reflect that Hades is in all probability a hotter spot, they invariably begin to ponder over the chances of saving their souls. An illustrated tale always fixes itself upon the mind more indelibly than one plainly printed without such assistance. Noumea is for the most part built upon land reclaimed

from the foreshores of the harbour. Many
of the wealthier inhabitants have erected for
themselves cool and pleasant-looking residences upon the sides of the mountain wall
at the rear of the town, where also is situated
the gubernatorial residence, in the centre of
a most charming tropical plantation.

Proportionately to the number of its
population, Noumea probably possesses more
cafés and liquid-refreshment rooms than any
other town in creation. There are over sixty
licensed houses in the place, and drinking
appears to be indulged in to an almost alarming extent by the thirsty population. Upon
Sunday, which, as is well known, is recognised as a gay and festive holiday by French
people generally, the cafés and saloons are
all open, and yet one meets with less drunken-
ness than is encountered in the towns in
Australia and New Zealand, where, in most
cases, the hotels and public-houses are closed
by law from Saturday night till Monday
morning.

The Sabbath Day is more sombre and solemn-looking in Australia than it is even in England.   And Sunday is more gay and rollicking in Noumea than it is even in France.   Imagine, then, with what strange feelings the Australian on his first visit to the capital of the great French penal colony strolls out on a Sunday afternoon to find a cricket match going on in the public gardens, a band gaily playing the liveliest dance music, and the bar-rooms crowded with people on all sides of him.   And he will search the streets in vain on Sunday evening to find a drunken man or to see a row.   Is it that the French people conduct themselves better under the influence of liquor than the average Englishman or Australian, or is it that they can 'carry' it better?   Or do the Australian prohibitive regulations excite the obstinacy of the otherwise genial colonist, and engender a desire in his bosom to make a big effort to procure liquor at all hazards, and to imbibe it largely when he does procure it, just for spite?

Sunday in Noumea is a day of rest—for
inveterate dancers only. And who does not
dance in the convict capital? On week
nights, immediately after dinner is got
through, the small round tables so profusely
scattered over the ground floors of the hotels
are removed, the band begins to play—a
small band is attached permanently to every
hostelry of any pretensions—and the dancers
come pouring in from different quarters.
Most of the public-houses are 'tropically'
built ; that is, the whole of the ground floor
is preserved as one room, with a small space
fenced off, in one of the corners, for the
purposes of a bar.

This serves as a dining-room and drinking
saloon during the day and a ball-room in the
evening. In the more fashionable rooms the
evening scene is a gay one indeed, as presented to the eye of the unsophisticated
traveller. Officers in their bright uniforms are
plentiful, pretty and dashingly-dressed women,
many of whom are pointed out to the stranger

as *libérés* who distinguished themselves in
the home country by their kleptomaniacal
proclivities, and young men and women of all
shades of colour, from the fascinating quad-
roon down to the dusky Kanaka of New
Caledonia.

The aboriginal of New Caledonia is a
curious customer.   He hates the Frenchman,
or ' Kai-oui-oui,' as fervently as his Satanic
Majesty hates holy water.   But convert him
into a policeman, drawing what is to him the
munificent pay of twenty-five francs per
month, and he is the most devoted servant
of the Republic, and the most abject syco-
phant, who bows before, or touches his cap
to, the passing citizen.   In his wild state the
Kanaka much resembles the Maori of New
Zealand in his surliness of temper and
general want of amiability, though little resembling him in colour or physical characteristics.   When he finds his way to a town,
such as Noumea, he affects the greatest
cordiality towards everybody but Frenchmen,

and he also adopts a good deal of the gesticu-
latory style of the latter, though certainly
without any intention of paying homage to
French customs.

As a policeman, he is a terror to peaceful
citizens as well as to evil-doers. A few years
since a young man from Adelaide was over
for a few months' visit to some friends in
Noumea. He was out visiting rather late
one evening, and on his return homewards,
as he was hurrying along one of the dark,
unlighted streets—they have not reached
street lamps in the convict capital yet—he
was accosted by a native policeman. Before
he had time to make any explanation the
policeman made an effort to handcuff him,
probably assuming, though very unreason-
ably, that he was a runaway convict. A
scuffle ensued, and the black commenced to
use the native wooden pickaxe with which
he was armed, and the consequence was that
the young fellow was killed upon the spot.
An inquiry was held, but of course without

any satisfactory result, as far as the friends of the murdered youth were concerned.

They have a kind of Bois de Bologne in Noumea, in which, when a duel is on the *tapis*, the battle is fought upon a Sunday morning.   Duels were rife in New Caledonia a few years ago.   They have fallen off a good deal lately, owing to interference on the part of the authorities.   A young fellow went over from Australia once to try his luck at business in the convict colony.   Like most new chums in every colony, he devoted a good deal of his time, and his money also, during the first few weeks, to seeing the sights of the capital.   Much of his time was spent among the cafés and billiard saloons, and, as a matter of course with a gay Australian Lothario, he became enamoured of some fair Hebe who dispensed absinthe and cocktails over one of the fashionable bars.   But he only happened to be one of many who had been softly sighing in that direction.   The numerous phalanx against

which he had to contend consisted solely of
Noumeans, and one of them very hotly
resented the intrusion of the stranger from
Botany Bay. At last the Australian threat-
ened to punch the Frenchman's head. This
was of course what might have been expected
from a vulgar fellow of English habits. The
use of the knuckle, especially in the excitement of love affairs, was indeed a degrading
and vulgar method to suggest. Next day
the Australian was waited upon at his hotel
by a friend of his rival, who invited him to
name a friend with whom the necessary pre-
liminaries for the duel could be arranged.
The Australian found at last that, however he might dislike the idea of fighting
another man with swords, he could not
possibly, with any show of decency, get out
of the difficulty. The meeting came off
in due course. The Australian, who had
scarcely ever seen a sword before, let alone
used one, was rather at a loss how he should
begin. However, probably before the

Frenchman was quite ready, he rolled into him pell-mell, and nearly chopped his head off before he could realise what was the matter. The duel ended here, and the Frenchman left the field minus an ear and with a terrible gash over his collar-bone, but armed with the firm resolve that when he fought again he should pick out an adversary who had some science about him, and who would go about the business properly, so as to give another scientific man a chance.

The Australian, however, flushed with his success, was quite anxious to have another go at someone. Without seeking far he was very soon accommodated. But his challenger on this occasion, not to be drawn into the sword business, proposed pistols as the weapons to be used. It was all the same to the Cornstalk. He had had some experience with the revolver, but to get his hand in he promptly purchased one, with a box of cartridges, and spent an afternoon in the woods at the back of the town, where he

was able to indulge in some quiet practice
on his own account. The consequence was
that at the meeting on the following Sunday
morning, at his first shot he lodged a bullet
in his adversary's thigh, and laid him up on
a bed from which he was unable to rise for
the next two months.

When a convict does happen to elude
the vigilance of his warders, which happens,
strange to say, very often, the policeman
who effects his capture obtains a reward of
fifty francs. To the Kanaka gendarme this
is a tempting amount, and as the Government pay the reward for the production of
the *évadé's* body, dead or alive, and as part
of the Kanaka's religion is to keep his own
skin as whole as possible, the unfortunate
runaway generally has a very rough time of
it in Noumea.

One day during my sojourn in Noumea
two policemen approached the place from the
direction of St. Louis, and as they came
down the winding road from the hillside

leading into the town it could be seen that they were carrying something between them on a pole. What at first appeared to be a prize in the shape of a captured bush-pig turned out upon a closer examination to be an *évadé* who had escaped from Noumea some days previously. He was rudely tied on to the pole which the men carried between them. Some humane people on the street remonstrated with the Kanakas when they deposited their burden on the pavement to indulge in a short rest. ‘Oh,’ replied one, ‘we were compelled to tie him tightly; he gave us a lot of trouble catching him, and we were fearful lest he might escape again.’ But when, later on, they deposited their burden in the prison dépôt on the Quay, it was found that the poor prisoner had indeed escaped. But the fifty francs were counted out all the same.

THE MISSIONARY IN THE SOUTH SEAS

IT is not many years since the first batch of missionaries went down to the sea in ships, and found landing places upon the lovely islands which are so profusely scattered over the Pacific. Early in the present century—somewhere about the time of Waterloo—the Rev. Mr. Henry found his way from England to the Society Islands (now known as Tahiti), and hoisted the flag of Christianity. Mr. Henry is the generally acknowledged pioneer of Christian labour in that part of the world, and the good work which he performed amongst the Tahitians was not, happily, interred with his bones, but lives after him.

The Tahitians are a gentle and tractable

people, and the popular Pacific Island custom of cannibalising was never very extensively developed amongst them. Consequently Mr. Henry had the distinction of living a long life there, and of dying a natural death in the end. This latter circumstance distinguishes the story of his life from that of the vast majority of his contemporaries, who, as a rule, died of a sudden.

In those groups of islands stretching along from the New Hebrides up towards the Solomons and New Guinea, boiled missionary was for many years, and in some places still is, the favourite dish. A plump young Englishman, who has been carefully reared, and has never had many opportunities of poisoning his blood and his flesh with alcoholic stimulants, comes out well in the cooking, when compared with the roystering gin-drinking islander who often finds his way to the oven after a battle amongst the tribes.

'Preparations for a South Sea island

dinner' would have been a splendid study
for the artist who could have looked on as
the Rev. Mr. Brown landed upon the shore
of Santa Cruz some years ago. The interested
natives had watched the boat drop anchor,
and each coco-nut tree that faced the unlucky
missionary as he strode confidently up the
beach concealed a dusky form and a formidable
club. The excitement was keen as the new
arrival walked forward in the direction of
the smoke which indicated the location of the
native village. The man behind the first tree
was 'warm' as the missionary passed within
a few feet of him. The next man was 'cold,'
Mr. Brown having walked out into the open.
He soon made one of the anxious islanders
'hot' by walking right up against his tree.
At short range a club never misses fire.
The poor missionary went the way of all
flesh in a most precipitous manner. And
the way of all human flesh on the Santa Cruz
was a merry one—merry, of course, for those
who accompanied it. Different portions of

the Rev. Mr. Brown found living tombs that day, and his skull is still retained by an old chief living up amongst the mountains. The chief happened to be in the village the day of the massacre, and was a spectator of the whole proceedings. Although he retains the head as a trophy, he was not the man who clubbed the missionary, and he also, strangely enough, refrained from partaking of the repast. The condition of the missionary was prime—so the chief was told by several people who were there. I have every reason to believe that the old man was innocent of any complicity in the proceedings, because he told me so himself, and I never knew a Santa Cruz chief to tell a lie yet, except to get money or gin out of me.

Before I commenced to travel I had a well-set idea that the preacher of the gospel, wherever he happened to be met, would of necessity be a very proper person indeed. If he smoked tobacco, or imbibed liquor, he would do it privately, always presenting to the outside world a good example of moral and abstemious conduct. How the idols of a boy's fancy are shivered and blasted when he pries into a few outside corners of the world! I was once cruising along the coast of Malayta when I ran into a small cove one evening for shelter. We made up to the town at the head of the harbour, and were guided by a native whom we met to the house of the village chief. Here we found a pleasant company assembled. Several gaily-painted chiefs and a white man occupied the mat of honour in the centre of the floor, deeply engaged in the classic study of draw-poker, and the air was filled with the seductive fragrance of gin-punch. The poker was abandoned, and a hearty welcome accorded to us, my countryman being very demonstrative in his gestures and words of greeting. I shall never forget him. He had many points about him which commended him to me as a good soul, for at sea we learn

L

to look charitably on the vagaries of a man
and a brother when we see any indication
that, whatever be his failings, his heart is in
the right place.

White men are mutually inquisitive in the
South Seas.   After he had pumped me dry
with questions as to where I hailed from,
whither I was bound, and the nature of my
business, I returned the compliment by asking him what he was doing on Malayta.   ' I
am the sky-pilot for this coast,' he replied
playfully.   This was my first experience of
a good healthy tobacco-chewing muscular
Christian, and I was rather amused and
entertained by the sample before me.   Of
rough personal exterior, he completed the
picture by affecting the slovenly dress of the
trader, with a few touches of native adorn-
ment added.   He wore a native cloth turban
on his otherwise bare head, and concealed
the greater portion of the rest of his body
with a regatta shirt and a pair of moleskin
pants.   I have mentioned that he was a good

soul, and his character shall, therefore, not be depreciated here.

One of his strong points was the utter absence from his mental composition of anything which could be construed into hypocrisy or bigotry. Another good point was that he was very plain-spoken. When the time came on for evening prayers one of the young fellows present—evidently a kind of pupil of the missionary—offered up the usual extempore prayer. The community was Wesleyan, and the young suppliant confined his application for Divine encouragement and clemency to the body of which he was a member. When he had concluded, the missionary, who had for a few moments been nervously handling a coco-nut which lay upon the mat beside him, sent the nut flying at the youth's head with unerring aim, at the same time remarking—' Didn't I tell you last night to give the Catholics a show ?'

The young fellow, rather sullenly, resumed his prayers, this time asking rather em-

phatically for a shower of heavenly blessings
on the head of the ' Kai Katolikas.'

I spent several days in the village, and
would have probably remained several weeks
in the enjoyment of my friend's pleasant
company were it not for the circumstance
that he was much my superior at poker
and euchre, and for the trifling additional
circumstance that he always insisted upon
having something on each game, just by
way of making it interesting. When one
dollar follows another in rapid and regular
succession without any break, for two or
three days, cards become monotonous, and I
decided to clear out from that port without
much delay. The game of poker, as it was
developed between the missionary and myself,
became merely a trial of Science *v.* Luck. I
played, and trusted to my luck, while my
friend based his play upon scientific rules.

The good and the bad are to be found
amongst all sorts and conditions of men. The
South Sea missionary body is no exception

in this respect. While there are many lame ducks, there are also amongst them men whose nobleness of purpose and heroism in the discharge of their oftentimes unpleasant and dangerous duties evoke the most unreserved admiration for their conduct.

On the occasion of the massacre of the wives of a late Fiji King—the prevailing custom upon the death of a king or chief— two white missionaries were stationed on the island of Bau, where the ceremony took place. While the necessary preparations were being made one of the missionaries offered the officiating murderers the alternative of cutting off his hand as an atonement for sparing the unfortunate women's lives. He tried very hard to induce them to accept this propitiatory sacrifice, but without success, probably because a white man's hand, however palatable and tasty, would not go round as well in a large dinner company as five or six bodies.

But while the majority of the missionaries

are impelled by a strong desire to carry out
their work with thoroughness and sincerity,
there are many whose natural proclivities are
of the earth, earthy. Take, for instance,
the 'sky-pilot' who combines business with
the pleasure of guiding souls in the way that
they should go. The trader-missionary has
a great. deal to answer for, if only for the
amount of Pacific blasphemy which he is
the cause of extracting from the legitimate
trader with whose business he interferes. If
you go on a trading expedition to a district
where one of this class of missionary shep-
herds the native flock, you require to be
very polite in your movements to insure any
success in your undertaking. During my
own trading experience in the South Seas the
line which I generally found the best to follow
was that of submitting a present to the missionary. The intrinsic value of the testimo-
nial would, of course, be regulated by the
amount of business likely to be done within
the jurisdiction of the 'sky-pilot' to whom it

was tendered. And sometimes a competitive lay trader would appear upon the scene, which rendered it necessary that he should, if possible, be outbid. Competition was a splendid thing for the missionary, who invariably temporised and hesitated till he extracted the highest possible bribe from the more enterprising of the two traders. The unlucky trader whose tender was not accepted withdrew from the place at once, as there was no use for him to stay in the face of the mandate from the missionary to the natives which followed the acceptance of the successful trader's bid.

In some cases the traders refuse to recognise the claims of the missionary to any royalty of the kind, but they invariably lose money by it. The sky-pilot has a tight grip on his followers.

THE CASTAWAYS

A TALE OF CANNIBALISM

THE Tokalau, or Line Islands, as they are more popularly known to travellers in the Pacific Ocean, from the circumstance that they lie directly under the Equator, consist of a numerous archipelago of small islets, or atolls, the largest of which is not more than thirty-five miles in length. Longitudinally these islands are situated to the northward of the Fiji group, between 174 degrees and 180 degrees east. They are inhabited by a curious race of people, called, from the islands on which they live, the Kai Tokalaus. ' Kai' is the generic Pacific term for man. A Frenchman is known to the natives as a Kai Oui Oui, an Englishman a Kai Piritania, a Jew a Kai Tierusalemi, and so on.

From their general physical characteristics one would incline to the conclusion that
the Kai Tokalaus are of Mongolian extrac-
tion ; they have no sentiment or poetry in
their composition, and it may be safely said
that they are the most debased set of aborigi-
nals existing in that part of the world. Of
a naturally savage and bloodthirsty nature,
they have made the Tokalau archipelago the
greatest martyr field for missionaries in
the South Seas. Cooked missionary often
figured upon the unwritten *menu* of the
festivals prepared for the island chieftains.
And how any of these devoted men have
managed to survive the risks and horrors of
the Line Islands, and accomplish the noble
results which have been attained amongst the
people, is a wonder to travellers.

Apart from their ferocious instincts, the
Tokalaus possess many curious personal
characteristics which are not to be generally
found in the other denizens of the Pacific
Islands. Not the least remarkable of these

is the uncontrollable desire to travel. Family
ties and bonds of affection have alike no
hold upon the Tokalau if an opportunity
presents itself by which he may travel abroad
—he does not care where ; if it be to the
farthest ends of the world it is all the same
to him. Without a word of adieu to his wife,
his children, or his parents, the Tokalau will
jump aboard a whaler for a three or four
years' voyage, and leave his home without
the faintest notion of ever returning to it
again. If chance brings him back after the
whaling voyage is over, well and good ; if
chance brings him instead to some remote
corner of the world, thousands of miles away
from the Tokalaus, it is all the same to
him.

When the writer was reluctantly compelled, through shipwreck, to spend fourteen
weeks upon one of the Tokalau islands, a few
years back, a strange incident occurred. A
party of eight of the islanders returned home
from a neighbouring archipelago, where they

had been dropped by a trading schooner, in which they had recently come from San Francisco. They had been away from home for a period of nearly three years, during the greater part of which they had been travelling. Their story was a strange account of suffering and adventure.

The Tokalaus are low islands, having been formed by degrees on the crests of a series of coral reefs—a common physical occurrence in the Pacific Ocean. None of the islands are more than six feet above sea level, and the coco-nut trees, with which the islands abound, although most prolific in the matter of fruit-bearing, are stunted in growth when compared with the general height of such trees.

The sea currents are also very rapid and treacherous in these regions. Hence, in passing from one island to another in small boats or native canoes, the *voyageur* often loses sight of land, and when particular attention is not paid to the tide rip, or the current, there is a considerable risk of being carried away to sea.

Nearly three years before the return of these eight survivors a mixed party of twenty-two Tokalaus—men, women, and children—started one afternoon from a mission station on one of the islands to visit the missionary on a neighbouring atoll. They sailed away before a very mild breeze in the whaleboat belonging to the mission. When they got well away from the land—out of sight of it, in fact—the breeze had almost died away. The sail was kept up, however —a thing which the Tokalau will always do while there is an ounce of wind to blow him along. He does not believe in doing with the oar, in a hot climate, what a thoughtful Providence will do for him with a few puffs of wind. And the matter of time is no object to the Tokalau.

The consequence was that night came upon the party while they were yet tossing gently about on the glassy water, many miles from home and from their point of destination. The treacherous current had also been doing its work, and when, after a weary night had been passed, day again dawned upon them, they were far away from any chance of reaching land—for some time at all events. Unacquainted, of course, in the absence of landmarks, with their position upon the ocean, and confused as to the course which they ought to steer, the wildest disorder began to reign amongst them.

One steered in the direction which he thought the right one for a few hours, when, no land appearing ahead, he was violently ejected from his place at the tiller and re-placed by one who thought he knew better. The boat was steered to all points of the compass, till at last the most sensible plan under the circumstances was resorted to— that of sailing away before the wind—going, in fact, wherever the wind had a mind to take them. The new course was no sooner proposed than it was unanimously adopted, holding out, as it did, the prospect of an adventure in some foreign country—a prospect dear to the Tokalau's heart. The prevailing breeze in the Pacific during the greater portion of the year is from the southeast, and this breeze happened to be blowing at the period of the adventurers' resolve to sail before the wind. Days and weeks passed, and still they flew away before it, without, however, meeting with the slightest sight of land. The small amount of provisions which they had originally carried aboard had been long since exhausted, and the greatest trouble now in the immediate front of them was hunger. But to a set of cannibals a way out of such a difficulty was not long in suggesting itself. It was merely a case of the survival of the fittest. The weakest of the party went first. The young people were sacrificed, one by one, to satisfy the hungry cravings of the older and stronger ones. After the young and tender ones had been used up, the turn of the unfortunate women came. The greatest economy in the use of the food was exercised, probably in recognition of the well-known human instinct that self-preservation is the first law of nature. And when at last the number of the whaleboat's occupants had dwindled down from twenty-two to eight, land was sighted ahead one morning. No accurate account had been kept of the time the adventurers had been at sea, but the period occupied must have been at least seven or eight weeks, for when they landed they found themselves upon the coast of Japan, some thousands of miles away from the Tokalau group. It may be imagined that the travellers created no small amount of astonishment and interest amongst the Japanese whom they first encountered. Taking note of the somewhat Mongolian features of the Kai Tokalaus, it is only natural that they were mistaken for some outlandish Chinese natives who had wandered across, or been reluctantly driven across, the Chinese Sea. It was, of course, impossible for them to make themselves understood, except by gestures, and, after much parleying by that primitive method, they were eventually conveyed to one of the mission stations along the coast, where the good and patient missionaries, full of information regarding the mission work and the inhabitants of the Pacific, were able at last to discover that their unfortunate guests came from the Tokalau archipelago. They were retained at the station for some time, till an opportunity at last presented itself, when passages were secured for them upon a sailing vessel bound from Yokohama to San Francisco. The latter port, though far from being in the direction of home, would offer them many chances of reshipping in the direction of their own country, as a large number of trading vessels ply between 'Frisco and the Pacific Islands.

In due time the adventurers passed through the celebrated Golden Gate, and

were landed in San Francisco. Here their
first care was, of course, to endeavour to
secure passages in the direction of their
home under the Equator. They were fortunate enough at last to get over one stage
of the journey through getting berths on a
vessel bound to Honolulu, the capital of the
Sandwich Islands.

At Honolulu they fell into the hands
of an enterprising American showman, who
promptly opened negotiations with them to
show for a brief season in San Francisco.
The affair seemed genuine, as money was
forthcoming, and back they went to the
Californian capital in charge of the showman, who exhibited them there for a considerable time, and with the greatest success,
as 'wild men from the interior of Thibet.'
They brought back with them many of the
bills and posters through which they had
been advertised to the American public, and
probably retain them yet as mementoes of
their curious adventure. The showman

appears to have behaved very handsomely towards them, and when the engagement came to a conclusion they were well supplied with funds and other necessaries, and a passage secured for them upon the trading schooner which eventually landed them in the neighbourhood of the Tokalaus.

The islanders had, of course, long since given them up as dead, and a few of the survivors who had left wives behind returned to find the good ladies in possession of other husbands. This naturally caused some irritation, and the King of the island was called upon to King-Solomonise and otherwise adjudicate upon the matter.

Peace was restored when the writer left the place, but the Tokalaus had made up their minds that when they ventured upon the water again and the wind fell the order was to be—' Man the oars ! '

THE SANDWICH ISLANDS—THE LEPER COLONY OF MOLOKAI

MOST people remember the heroic conduct of Father Damien, the Belgian priest who voluntarily entombed himself among the lepers on the island of Molokai in 1873.

The kingdom of Hawaii will always hold a place in the minds of English people who care to dwell upon the travels and adventures of Captain James Cook. Loyal Englishmen, whose pride is the vastness of our great Empire—upon which it has been truly said that the sun never sets—whose pride it is also to remember that our Colonial subjects are, if possible, more strong and enthusiastic than the people at home in their devotion to the Throne and their desire to uphold and maintain the integrity and the unity of the

British Empire, will always be prepared to acknowledge the indebtedness of that Empire to the labours of James Cook.

The Sandwich Islands were first touched by Captain Cook in 1778, and thus named by him, in honour of his patron, the Earl of Sandwich, who occupied the position of First Lord of the Admiralty at that time. This name is, however, gradually being dropped, and probably it is much better that the original native name should be perpetuated. Such a change has actually taken place in most of the other archipelagos in the Pacific to which English names were given by Captain Cook and other navigators. The Society Islands—so called by Cook on account of the social and hospitable characteristics of the islanders—are now universally spoken of as the Tahitian Islands.

It is understood, by the way, that the social pre-eminence of the Tahitians consisted simply in the circumstance that cannibalism was not indulged in by the islanders.

The Friendly Islands, the Navigators, and the Cannibal Islands have now totally dropped those titles, and are known to travellers by their old native names of Tonga, Samoa, and Fiji respectively.

The kingdom of Hawaii consists of eight islands : Hawaii, Maui, Kahulaui, Lanai, Molokai, Oahu, Kauai, and Niihau.

The superficial area of the whole group is over 6,000 square miles. A large proportion of this area is covered with volcanic scoriæ and pumice, rendering it unfit for agricultural purposes ; but that portion which is available to the planter is not to be surpassed in any part of the Pacific, or indeed in any part of the tropical world, for richness and producing capacity. When the late George Augustus Sala passed through Honolulu he was struck with the remarkable fertility of the place, which he called in some of his papers the ' Eden ' of the Pacific. Or, to quote the chatty journalist more fully, he spoke of Hawaii as the ' Eden and the

Serpent.' The 'serpent' was a graphic point at the hideous disease of leprosy which has for years been crawling about amongst the people of these fairy islands.

Although this dreadful disease was—to a very limited extent only—known to the natives of most of the Pacific Islands before the advent of foreigners, there is no doubt that, in the case of Hawaii and the Tahitian Islands, the alarming spread of the disease of late years is more directly traceable to the Chinese labour immigrants who have been introduced from Macao and Canton.

The Hawaiian will avoid hard work as persistently as any of his coloured brethren of the Pacific, and that is saying a great deal. And it will surprise no one who has travelled amongst the islands that such is the case. Providence is peculiarly kind to the islander:

The Kava feast, the yam, the coco-root,
Which bears at once the cup, the milk, the fruit ;
The bread-tree, which, without the ploughshare, yields
The unreap'd harvest of unfurrowed fields,
And bakes its unadulterated loaves
Without a furnace in unpurchas'd groves.

These are the natural perquisites of the Pacific islander. In the matter of fish and other kindred delicacies, the pleasure of catching them is the peculiar prerogative of woman. And the man takes a pleasure in letting her do it. Everything is placed to the native's hand, without any effort on his part to obtain it. There are a good many people outside of the Pacific who would not hanker much after work if they could get all the necessaries of life upon such terms.

Such being the state of affairs among the islands, the white coffee, tea, or sugar planter is invariably compelled to introduce foreign labour to his estates. During the past twenty or thirty years large drafts have been imported from China and India for the estates in Hawaii. The labour-recruiters in Calcutta, Macao, and Canton were not very particular as to the class of people whom they engaged —in fact, for the greater part they could not afford to be—where the wages offered were only at the rate of about 10 dollars per annum.

Hence the slums of these pestilential cities were drawn upon for the required labourers, and before the immigration system had been long in force at Honolulu that lovely spot was reeking with the accursed plague of leprosy.

The island of Molokai, which lies between Oahu and Maui, and not far from Honolulu, was selected by the Government for use as a quarantine ground to which to transmit persons affected with the disease. When a case is discovered the patient is placed in a small native canoe, or a boat which is of little value. In this he is towed by a steamer or sailing vessel to the shores of Molokai, where he is cut adrift and allowed to make his way ashore as best he can.

Years ago I paid several visits to Molokai, and on one occasion the little colony of lepers were in a deplorable condition, in consequence of the inclemency of the season. There are several settlements, or townships, on the island, and the communal system of

living, so common to Pacific Island peoples,
is much in vogue amongst the lepers.

Of course, the large majority of the
residents on Molokai are but slightly affected
with the disease, and in many cases leprosy
develops very slowly. But the measures
which the Honolulu Government found it
necessary to adopt for the suppression of
leprosy were of such a drastic kind that the
slightest symptoms of the disease were suffi-
cient to warrant the banishment of the
unfortunate subject.

One Englishman, who was well known
some years ago in Hawaiian political circles
—who had, in fact, held an important legal
position in the Government at one period—
had the misfortune to become slightly affected by leprosy in one of his hands. He
wore gloves—an unusual thing in Honolulu
—for some time to conceal the terrible white
spot from public view. But the gloves
attracted suspicion, and the 'leper detec-
tives' made a raid upon him. Through his

social position and his general popularity,
many efforts were made to get him away
in outgoing vessels for America or the
Chinese side, but he was eventually cut
adrift from a Government vessel off Molokai. When I last saw him he had got
into considerable practice in his profession
amongst the lepers, but the scale of fees was
somewhat different to that which he had
been in the habit of charging in Honolulu
and New Zealand. His position was also
more in the character of a judge than an
advocate. He had just adjudicated in an
important breach of promise case between
two patients, and, having decided that the
would-be deceiver should marry the girl, the
worthy lawyer was inundated with fees in
the shape of bunches of bananas, baskets of
yams, coco-nuts, &c., supplied for the most
part by the girl's friends and admirers.

In some cases, when the judge obtains
fees which appear to be too much in excess

of what is reasonable, the chief missionary extemporises himself into a prothonotary, and taxes the costs. This little piece of business is always carried out with the utmost good humour on the part of the two parties most immediately concerned, and the quantity by which the costs are reduced is conveyed to the missionary's residence, from which it may be needless to say it is not again sent into circulation.

Molokai contains about a thousand inhabitants. Plantation work of all kinds is followed by the majority of the people, who inter-marry and otherwise follow out all the social customs to which they have been reared.

A severe season naturally affects them more than it would a robust class of people. I remember some of the villages being in a terrible state. The people had become so reduced as to be unable to help one another, and all the work, of course, fell upon the late famous Father Damien. The large numbers of the residents who were lucky enough not to be seriously affected were unwilling to go amongst the stricken villagers and thus risk a more virulent contagion than they already had.

It would be hard indeed—if at all possible—to imagine a scene of greater horror and loathsomeness than the picture of a leper village of low degree, such as those which are often to be seen upon Molokai. The writer had the somewhat grim distinction of riding over Isandlwanha when that blood-marked spot was but a few days known to fame, but the remembrance of it is sweet in comparison with the ghastliness of Molokai.

That men can be found to stand up and die game amidst the terrors of such work as Isandlwanha witnessed ; that men can be found who are prepared to face any danger which the imagination can conjure up on

flood or field, we already know; but it was
a new departure in heroism when young
Damien voluntarily abjured a life of promise
and comparative luxury to devote the remainder of his days to the misery of an
existence in pestilential Molokai.

A MODEL MONARCH

TIAOJI TUBOU, KING OF TONGA

THE Tongans are generally admitted to be among the smartest people in the Pacific. They have more self-reliance and natural ability as a rule than the other Pacific islanders, with the exception, of course, of the Maoris, and it has been a matter of general interest to watch the developments that have taken place in the Tongan archipelago in recent years. One of the most striking figures in the public life of the South Pacific during the latter half of this century has undoubtedly been the late King George of Tongatabu. Although anything but a warlike or ambitious man, King George, from the time that he ascended the throne of Tonga up till the moment of his death, held the most prominent place in the public eye in the Pacific, and his word was law to many chiefs and peoples outside the limited archipelago over which he legally ruled.

Tiaoji Tubou, to give him his Tongan name, was born in 1796, so that he had nearly reached his century when he died in 1893. Like many another Tongan chief, Tiaoji Tubou left his native country when quite a young man, to see the rest of the world for himself. Shipping on board a whaler, he knocked about a good deal in Australian and American parts before he returned to Tonga-tabu.

When he did return home he found a fierce rebellion going on against his family's dynasty, and having picked up a good deal of general knowledge during his wanderings, he was naturally looked to for aid in the suppression of the rising. He was a long time stamping out the trouble, but stamp it out he did in a most effective way, and during the campaign earned a great reputation for per-

sonal. deeds of valour and generally for his
prudence and courage in the command of
fighting men.   He ascended the throne of
Tonga on December 4, 1845, and his modera-
tion was aptly exemplified in connection with
the enthroning function, as he insisted on
doing away with all the grotesque ceremony
which usually marked such occasions, simply
celebrating his ascension to the throne by
holding a comparatively informal kava meeting.   In other words, the new king invited
his friends and supporters simply to come and
have a drink with him on the strength of his
accession.   After he had been at the head of
affairs in Tonga for a short time, the Wesleyan
missionaries induced him to become a member
of that religious body, and as he took up
Christianity with abnormal enthusiasm for a
Polynesian prince, he soon became what is
called a lay-preacher in that body.   For a
number of years he occupied the pulpit
regularly, and, as may be imagined, he was a
great draw as a preacher.   In 1853, shortly

after the discovery of gold in Australia, King
George went over to Sydney, with the idea,
so it was said, of taking up some gold lands
and working them with the cheap labour
which he could bring over from Tonga.
Either the plan was not found feasible under
the existing labour regulations, or the king
himself did not care to tackle the hardships
attending life on the then very wild gold-fields,
at any rate he returned to Tonga and quietly
worked away at his own gold-mine, the tax-
ation of the Tonga people. It was shortly
after this that King George paid a visit to the
late King Cakobau of Fiji, whom he eventually succeeded in converting from his well-
known wicked practices to a Christian life.
Cakobau had every reason to be grateful to
King George of Tonga for other things
besides his conversion to Christianity. On
one occasion, when a dangerous rebellion
broke out in Fiji which Cakobau found himself utterly unable to suppress, King George
sailed across from Tongatabu with a large

N

force of Tongan warriors and helped the Bau ruler out of his difficulties. On the whole King George was a dignified and large-hearted man of the world to whom the ruling of 25,000 or 30,000 people like the Tongans was an easy and congenial task. In the latter years of his life he was brought into much tribulation by the machinations of wicked whites who had settled in his country, and one of these, a well-known missionary, had eventually to be deported from Tongatabu by order of the British High Commissioner for the Western Pacific. The king was much beloved by all who knew him, and his death was the occasion for an expression of profound regret from one side of the South Pacific to the other.

PRINTED BY
SPOTTISWOODE AND CO., NEW-STREET SQUARE
LONDON

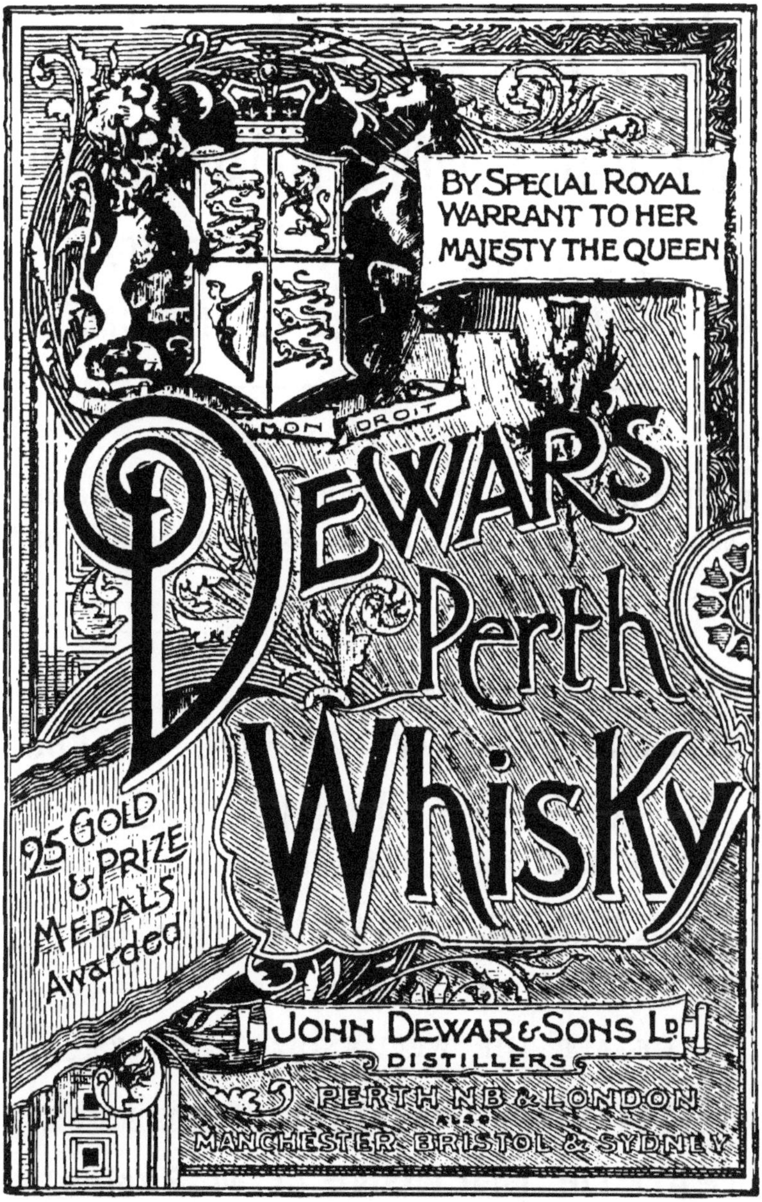
BY SPECIAL ROYAL WARRANT TO HER MAJESTY THE QUEEN
MON DROIT
DEWAR'S
Perth
Whisky
25 GOLD & PRIZE MEDALS Awarded
JOHN DEWAR & SONS Ld
DISTILLERS
PERTH NB & LONDON
ALSO
MANCHESTER BRISTOL & SYDNEY

W. BEST AND SONS,

Wine, Spirit, & Mineral Water Merchants,

22 HENRIETTA STREET,
CAVENDISH SQUARE, LONDON, W.

LONDON AGENTS FOR

R. Ellis & Sons' (Ruthin, North Wales) Table Waters,
Soda, Seltzer, Potass, Lithia, &c., in Bottles and
Syphons.

ALSO IMPORTERS OF ALL

NATURAL FOREIGN MINERAL WATERS.

CHAMPAGNE

(Deutz & Geldermann, Roper Frères, and others);

CLARETS,   HOCKS,   PORTS,

SHERRIES,   &c.

OF ALL THE WELL-KNOWN SHIPPERS.

VINUM EUCHARISTICUM (Communion Wine),
EAU DE COLOGNE (J. M. Farina).

*Price List of all Wines, Spirits, Liqueurs, and Beers forwarded
on application.*

THE BOOK OF THE SEASON.

SECOND EDITION.

SNAKES.

By 'SUNDOWNER.'

The Daily News.—'A pleasant little volume—might have been signed by "Truthful James" instead of by "Sundowner."'

Lancaster Standard.—'The book is an interesting production, anecdotal, brightly written, racy and entertaining to the superlative degree . . . thoroughly readable and worth purchasing.'

Financial News.—'Really good reading.'

Devon and Exeter Gazette.—'Although the sensitive reader of "Snakes" may feel a creeping sensation when perusing the accounts of "Sundowner's" thrilling experiences of that species of reptiles in Australia and Fiji, yet he or she cannot fail to be intensely interested by them. So extraordinary are some of the stories related that one might almost be inclined to question their genuineness, but, according to the preface, the book is intended as an antidote to "many unreliable and obviously fanciful accounts of snakes and their habits."'

The Scotsman.—'A study of the Australian and Fijian snakes, made by a writer who appears to have had considerable experience as a snake-farmer. The stories it tells are interesting in themselves, and, unlike the majority of snake stories that have got into print, do not bear upon their face a guarantee of their untruthfulness. The book is interesting, chatty, and well-informed, and will both amuse and instruct anyone who desires to have unsystematised information on its subject.'

Gall's News Letter.—'The author gives some of his own experiences with snakes. The elusive character of the reptile is first set forth; their occasional good deeds; the tragic end of one is dwelt upon in the first chapter in a manner that will certainly bear re-reading. We never realised until now how fond a snake is of music, nor of its wonderful power of digestion. The book shows an immense amount of study, and is written in a manner calculated to impress the reader.'

Daily Chronicle.—'We have read this book through from cover to cover, and cannot for the life of us make out whether it is meant as a huge and long-drawn joke, ophidian in length and coiliness, or whether it is supposed to be a contribution to snake history tempered by jocularity.'

Morning Advertiser.—'Not only instructive, but most entertaining.'

The Eastern Morning News.—'This is a second edition of a volume of stories illustrative of the habits and peculiarities of Australian and Fijian snakes. "Sundowner" is evidently an expert in spinning yarns of an amusing and extraordinary character; consequently "Snakes" is a book that the average boy will fully appreciate and enjoy. The ordinary reader will, however, scarcely be sufficiently credulous to accept the statements contained therein as absolute facts, but that circumstance need not interfere with their hearty appreciation of the humour of the book. "Snakes" will probably command a ready sale, as the lively style of the writer cannot fail to be appreciated.'

Weekly Irish Times.—'It is doubtful if the aspirant ophiologist will obtain much reliable information from this amusing volume. We say this in spite of "Sundowner's" declaration in the preface as to the veracity of the contents of his book, for a perusal of the many wonderful stories he tells will not, we fear, do much to clear away the doubt and suspicion with which the average snake story is regarded. But, taken as half joke or all joke, "Sundowner's" book is well worth reading, and, even if we refuse to believe the author's most stirring contribution to natural history, we must admire him for his sense of humour and frequent defiance of the limits of his reader's credulity.'

Published at the Offices of The European Mail (Limited),
Imperial Buildings, Ludgate Circus, London, E.C.

BRITISH EMPIRE LEAGUE,

BOTOLPH HOUSE, EASTCHEAP, LONDON, E.C.

The primary object of the League is to secure the permanent Unity of the Empire.

Minimum Subscription of Membership, One Guinea per Annum.

THE
Colonial College & Training Farms, Ld.,
HOLLESLEY BAY, SUFFOLK.

THE College provides for Youths intending to emigrate such practical training as will test their fitness and qualify them for Colonial life.

It is situated on its own Estate in a fine position on the sea coast.

Farms of over 1,800 acres are carried on by the College, which thus affords to its students unrivalled facilities for becoming practically, as well as theoretically, acquainted with all branches of Agriculture, and with Horse, Cattle, and Sheep breeding, &c., on a large scale.

Instruction is also regularly given in Dairying, Veterinary Science and Practice, Gardening, Surveying and Building Construction, Smith's, Carpenter's, Wheelwright's, and Harnessmaker's work, Riding, Ambulance, and various other subjects necessary to the young Colonist.

Many Students of the College are settled in almost every part of the Empire, with whom, as well as with other trustworthy correspondents able to render valuable assistance to new comers, regular communication is kept up.

Prospectus on application to the Resident Director at above address, or from 6 Victoria Street (Westminster Palace Hotel), S.W.

Mappin & Webb

MANUFACTURERS,

FACING THE MANSION HOUSE,

AND

158 to 162 OXFORD STREET,

LONDON, W.

MANUFACTORY—

ROYAL CUTLERY PLATE WORKS, SHEFFIELD.

Princes Plate, Reg. No. 71,552.

⯐ ⯐ Table Cutlery.

Spoons and Forks.

HIGHEST QUALITY.

---

25 Years Wear Guaranteed.

O 2

WESTERN AUSTRALIA

BY STEAM.

——— •••• ———

LOWEST RATES OF FREIGHT AND PASSAGE

FROM

London and *Liverpool,*

VIÂ CAPE AND VIÂ CANAL.

Steamers also calling at all Ports adjacent to

THE NORTHERN GOLD FIELDS.

APPLY—

W. MARDEN, 14 Fenchurch Street;

TRINDER, ANDERSON & CO., 4 St. Mary Axe;

BETHELL, GWYN & CO., 22 Billiter Street, E.C.

CANADIAN PACIFIC RAILWAY

AND

ROYAL MAIL STEAMSHIP LINE.

JAPAN AND CHINA.

The only actual Trans-Continental Railway on the American Continent. The longest line under one Management in the World. Its Trains and Steamers extend in a direct line from Atlantic tide-water to Hong-Kong—9,180 miles.

WANTED IN CANADA—Farmers, Farm-labourers, Domestic Servants, and Men willing to learn Farming. England's nearest Colony. Free 160-Acre Government Grants. Cheap Railway Lands. Good Markets. Free Schools.

JAPAN, CHINA, AUSTRALIA, NEW ZEALAND, ROUND THE WORLD. New Fast Passenger Service, *via* Vancouver. By best Atlantic Steamers, any line, to Quebec, Montreal, New York, Boston, or Halifax; thence *via* Canadian Pacific Railway, taking in Niagara Falls and the grand scenery of the Rockies. Only line running through-trains under one management Atlantic to Pacific.

EMPRESS OF INDIA, EMPRESS OF JAPAN, EMPRESS OF CHINA, 6,000 tons gross, 10,000 horse-power; largest, fastest, finest, only twin-screw steamers on the Pacific Ocean, leave Vancouver monthly for Japan and China, *via* Inland Sea.

Canadian-Australian Line Steamships, fastest and finest running from American Continent to Australasia, leave Vancouver monthly for Honolulu, Fiji, and Sydney. Electric Light. Good Cuisine. Exceptionally Large Cabins.

Round the World, *via* Japan and China, or Australia, or Africa.

CHEAP TOURS ON THE C.P.R. Cost less than a Continental Trip. More Luxurious. Fewer Extras. Express Train Service to Fishing and Shooting Grounds. Through the Finest Scenery in the World—an Enchanting Panorama of Lakes, Prairies, Mountains, and Rivers.

Everyone who reads this should apply personally or by letter for gratuitous and post-free accurate maps and handsomely illustrated guide-books. Various sets of pamphlets describing services, &c., as above, are published. State which set is required.

CANADIAN PACIFIC RAILWAY,
67 & 68 KING WILLIAM ST., LONDON, E.C.
30 Cockspur Street, | 7 James Street, Liverpool.
Charing Cross, S.W. | 67 St. Vincent Street, Glasgow.

UNION STEAMSHIP COMPANY

THE STEAMERS of the UNION LINE, comprising a Fleet of over 50 Vessels, have almost a world-wide reputation for Splendour, Comfort, Luxury, Cuisine, Speed, and everything that makes a sea voyage enjoyable.

THE COMPANY'S FINE STEAMERS RUN REGULARLY AS FOLLOWS:—

FROM MELBOURNE.—Weekly for all New Zealand Ports, calling at Hobart.

FROM SYDNEY.—Weekly for all East Coast Ports of New Zealand, also Weekly *viâ* Cook Strait and Wellington.

AUSTRALIA AND TASMANIA.—The Company has a Fleet of Steamers employed exclusively in running Services between Australia and Tasmania at frequent and regular intervals.

NEW ZEALAND SERVICES.—The bulk of the Company's Fleet is engaged in the Coastal Service of the Colony, and between the principal Ports there is almost daily communication.

SOUTH SEA ISLANDS SERVICE.—In addition to the foregoing Services, Steamers leave Auckland and Sydney monthly for the Island Groups of Fiji, Samoa, and Tonga, also for Raratonga and Tahiti. Tourists therefore enjoy facilities for

VISITING THE CORAL ISLANDS OF THE PACIFIC THE WHOLE YEAR ROUND.

Saloon Excursion Ticket from Auckland or Sydney, through the South Sea Islands, £20 to £25, according to route selected.

Head Office: DUNEDIN, NEW ZEALAND.
Branches at all principal Australian and New Zealand Ports.

OF NEW ZEALAND, LIMITED.

NEW ZEALAND EXCURSIONS.

Special facilities are provided for Tourists travelling round the Coast during the summer months, and a series of Special Excursions to the

WEST COAST SOUNDS

is arranged to sail from Dunedin in January of each year.

Each Trip will occupy about Nine Days from Port Chalmers, during which the most attractive of the Sounds will be visited, and special facilities will be given for FISHING, SHOOTING, and SKETCHING, and for exploring those wonderful Fiords, where Nature is seen in her grandest aspects. Opportunity will also be given for visiting THE SUTHERLAND FALLS—the Largest in the World—the Steamer remaining Two Days in Milford Sound for that purpose.

THE SOCIAL ENJOYMENT OF PASSENGERS

is made a special feature of these Excursions, the whole Trip taking the form of an extended picnic.

ROYAL MAIL SERVICE TO GREAT BRITAIN
VIÂ SAN FRANCISCO
(A. & A. ROUTE).

The Steamers of this Line—MONOWAI (3,433 tons), ALAMEDA (3,000 tons), MARIPOSA (3,000 tons)

Leave Sydney every FOURTH MONDAY for

AUCKLAND, APIA, HONOLULU, & SAN FRANCISCO,

And return from latter Port every FOURTH THURSDAY.

This is *the* Passenger Route to the Colonies, avoiding alike the heat of the Red Sea and the cold of Cape Horn, and giving passengers the opportunity of travelling in luxury and comfort through the most interesting country in the world.

THROUGH FIRST-CLASS FARE.—Sydney or Auckland to London, and *vice versâ*, £63. to £67. 8s.; Sydney or Auckland to San Francisco, and *vice versâ*, Saloon, £40; Sydney or Auckland to Honolulu, and *vice versâ*, Saloon, £30.

ROUND THE WORLD TOUR (First-class all the way), returning by Orient or P. and O. Co.'s Line from London *via* Suez; or by New Zealand Shipping Co. or Shaw, Savill and Albion Co.'s Line direct to New Zealand, or *vice versâ*, £125.

London Office: 34 LEADENHALL STREET.

SAN FRANCISCO: Messrs. J. D. SPRECKELS & BROS., Limited.

Egypt, Ralph C. Grafton, Esq., Ramleh, Alexandria.
Fiji, Hemliton-Hunter, Esq., Suva.
Hong-Kong, Hon. T. H. Whitehead, M.L.B.
Jamaica, Hon. C. S. Farquharson, M.L.C., Savanna-la-mar.
The Leeward Islands, Hon. W. H. Whyham, M.L.C., Antigua.
Malta, Hon. Count Strickland, C.M.G., Valetta.
Mashonaland, A. H. F. Duncan, Esq., Salisbury.
Mauritius, A. De Boucherville, Esq., Port Louis.
Natal, John Goodliffe, Esq., Durban.
New South Wales, W. L. Docker, Esq., Sydney.
New Zealand, James Allen, Esq., M.H.R., Dunedin.
,,   George Beetham, Esq., Wellington.

New Zealand, Hon. C. C. Bowen, M.L.C., Middleton, Christchurch.
,,   Douglas McLean, Esq., Napier.
,,   Auckland.
Queensland, Hon. Walter H. Wilson, M.L.C., Brisbane.
Sierra Leone, T. J. Alldridge, Esq., Sherbro'.
South Australia, George W. Hawkes, Esq., J.P., Adelaide.
Straits Settlements, A. P. Talbot, Esq., Singapore.
Tasmania, N. E. Lewis, M.A., Esq., B.C.L., M.H.A., Hobart.
Transvaal, W. T. Graham, Esq., Johannesburg.
Trinidad, Hon. H. W. Chantrell.
Victoria, Benjamin Cowderoy, Esq., Melbourne.
Western Australia, James Morrison, Esq., J.P., Guildford.

The Objects of the Institute are:—

' To provide a place of meeting for all gentlemen connected with the Colonies and British India, and others taking an interest in Colonial and Indian affairs ; to establish a reading room and library, in which recent and authentic intelligence upon Colonial and Indian subjects may be constantly available, and a Museum for the collection and exhibition of Colonial and Indian productions ; to facilitate interchange of experiences amongst persons representing all the dependencies of Great Britain ; to afford opportunities for the reading of papers, and for holding discussions upon Colonial and Indian subjects generally : and to undertake scientific, literary, and statistical investigations in connection with the British Empire. But no paper shall be read, or any discussion be permitted to take place, tending to give to the Institute a party character.' (Rule 1.)

There are two classes of fellows (who must be British subjects), resident and non-resident, both elected by the Council on the nomination of two fellows, one of whom at least must sign on personal knowledge. The former pay an entrance fee of £3, and an annual subscription of £2 ; the latter an entrance fee of £1. 1s. (which is increased to £3 when taking up permanent residence in the United Kingdom), and an annual subscription of £1. 1s. (which is increased to £2 when in the United Kingdom for more than three months). Resident fellows can compound for the annual subscription by the payment of £20, or after five years' annual subscription of £2, on payment of £15 ; and non-resident fellows can compound for the non-resident annual subscription on payment of £10.

The privileges of fellows, whose subscriptions are not in arrear, include the use of rooms, papers, and library. All fellows, whether residing in England or the Colonies, have a copy of the monthly journal, containing a report of each meeting, and the annual volume of proceedings forwarded to them.

To be present at the evening meetings, and to introduce one visitor.

To be present at the Annual Conversazione, and to introduce a lady.

The Institute occupies its own house, which is open on week-days from 10 to 8 p.m., and comprises library, reading, news rooms, writing rooms, offices, &c. The library, of 26.000 volumes (including pamphlets), chiefly on Colonial subjects. Books may be borrowed, and visitors introduced by a fellow are admitted.

The Annual Meeting is held in February or March ; ordinary meetings are held at 8 p.m. on the second Tuesday (as a general rule) of the months from November to June, as well as occasional afternoon meetings, for the reading and discussion of papers. The number of members on 25th November, 1895, was 3,815.

THE BOOK OF THE SEASON.

SECOND EDITION.

SNAKES.

By 'SUNDOWNER.'

Price 1s.

The Overland Mail.—'To anyone likely to take an interest in the reptilic reminiscences of a modest and religiously-inclined member of the far-famed family of hatchet-throwers, we can recommend a little volume on "Snakes" and their peculiarities, just issued by *The European Mail.* The experiences of the author, "Sundowner"—own brother, we should opine, to "Truthful James," and a past master in the art of drawing the long-bow—are, to say the least, remarkable, and, but for the fact that he repeatedly and earnestly impresses upon us that he is a man of a truthful and a serious mind, one would be inclined to credit him with virtues tending in a somewhat different direction. . . . Whoever lays out a shilling on this humorous and amusing little *brochure* will have to thank its author for an hour's pleasant and lively reading, and will find no difficulty in believing his statement that he has "often been complimented on the accuracy and 'freshness' of the matter which he places before the public from time to time."'

African Review.—'Is full of interesting and exciting stories about reptiles in the Antipodes, and anyone in search of sensations, nightmares, and the like will find it a veritable widow's cruse in that line. A score or so of nightmares at a shilling are cheap.'

Edinburgh Evening News.—Is devoted to the ways and manners of the Australian snake in all his varieties. "Sundowner" is apparently versed in snakes, and those who like a good creepy subject, and are not over-critical as to a little use of the long-bow, will appreciate the book.'

South African Empire.—'One of the most valuable contributions to "Snakeology" that we have seen, and literally sparkles with fresh, and hitherto wholly unexpected, facts about a subject whose turns and twists the author has closely studied in Australia. . . . Interesting, chatty, and very funny.'

Public Opinion.—'It is possible to get a good and invigorating half hour's entertainment out of this volume. The serpent world is under a debt of gratitude to "Sundowner" for the graceful and complimentary recital of its sagacity.'

Introduction.—'"Sundowner's" genial and pleasantly written monograph on the habitat and characteristics of snakes has, we are pleased to observe, attained to the distinction of a second edition. The author, whether playful, hilarious, or serious, is always amusing and interesting, and is evidently *facile princeps* of this absorbing subject, which, as all the world knows, comes periodically to brighten a dreary press during the "big gooseberry" season. In this veracious chronicle of his own experience there is much of shrewd and wary observation, pithily expressed, and coloured by an amiable fancy for natural incident and local surrounding, as well as exciting incidents and hairbreadth escapes.'

Dominica Guardian.—'It is an interesting and well-informed little work, both amusing and instructive to those who would obtain information on the subject of which it treats. . . . Has created a favourable impression.'

Jamaica Post.—'This is a most enjoyable little book; and it would be impossible to take up a volume which would help to while away more pleasantly an idle hour or two. "Sundowner" is a humorist of the first water; and the fun of his remarks is all the greater because of the exceeding gravity and earnestness of his literary style. No professor's descriptions could be couched in more sober language; and yet the reader is kept smiling, or laughing, at the humour of the narrative from the first page to the last. Mark Twain has rarely done anything better than "Sundowner" in this little *brochure,* and we can cordially recommend it to all. Some of the incidents are screamingly funny; but the adventure with the black snake takes the cake.'

Published at the Offices of The European Mail (Limited),
Imperial Buildings, Ludgate Circus, London, E.C.

www.ingramcontent.com/pod-product-compliance
Lightning Source LLC
Chambersburg PA
CBHW031058280326
41928CB00049B/980